MOMUS is the artist name of Nic in 1960. Educated at the Edinb Sir Walter Scott essay prize) alongside Ali Smith, he graduat he has lived in Athens, Mon Berlin, Tokyo and Osaka. His musical career as the song... Momus began in 1981 when he formed a group from the ashes of Edinburgh's legendary Postcard Records group Josef K. As a solo artist he's released more than 30 albums of satirical electronic folk music on independent labels like Creation and Cherry Red, as well as publishing six books of speculative fiction. In the art world he's best known for his performances as 'the unreliable tour guide', a museum docent who tells lies about painting and sculpture.

The Book of Scotlands

MOMUS

Luath Press Limited
EDINBURGH
www.luath.co.uk

First published by Sternberg Press 2009
This edition 2018
Reprinted 2020
Reprinted 2021

ISBN: 978-1-912147-43-4

The author's right to be identified as author of this book
under the Copyright, Designs and Patents Act 1988 has been asserted.

The paper used in this book is recyclable. It is made
from low chlorine pulps produced in a low energy, low emission
manner from renewable forests.

Printed and bound by Bell & Bain Ltd., Glasgow.

Typeset in 11 point Sabon

© Nick Currie 2018

Dedicated to Bill Currie,
angler and linguist, 1930–2015

Contents

Introduction by Gerry Hassan 9
Preface 15
Scotlands 19

Introduction to an Alternative Universe of Scotlands

Gerry Hassan

BOOKS AND WORDS define nations and times – and this is as true of Scotland as elsewhere. Some would argue that it is even more true of this nation. When people think of early 21st century Scotland years hence and ask who we were, what kind of people(s) were we, what were our hopes, fears and what drove our innermost emotions in relation to the book and the written word, many will cite the obvious volumes. These will include Tom Devine's *The Scottish Nation*, James Robertson's *And the Land Lay Still,* perhaps the detail and humanity of Kathleen Jamie's *Findings* – and, for a few, original historical books such as Catriona MacDonald's *Whaur Extremes Meet*.

Beyond these this wonderful, unique, strange collection by Momus, *The Book of Scotlands,* has the right to its very own special status and place. It takes us on a journey into a familiar landscape with many place names, people and histories that we know and feel we understand. But it uses them to take us somewhere utterly unfamiliar that is enchanting and spellbinding. We enter a Scotland of magic, surrealism, play and fun, which tells us something new about our country and the world, and where the author invites us to be a fellow traveller into this alternative universe of different Scotlands.

For those who need a short introduction to the world

of Momus – he is that rare and unusual creation, a genuine multi-talented polymath. Born Nick Currie in Paisley in 1960, he has lived in such varied places as Berlin, New York, Tokyo and Osaka. In 1981 he took the moniker 'Momus' from Greek mythology (where it denotes satire and mockery in *Aesop's Fables*), and whether relevant or not, there is a Herr Momus in Franz Kafka's *The Castle*.

Momus has been, and is, a singer-songwriter, writer and novelist, blogger, lecturer, performance artist, and art and design critic. Throughout all of these some consistent qualities have shone through. He has been described as 'Scotland's Morrissey' when that used to be seen as an unconditional positive, while more hilariously *MOJO* music magazine lauded him as 'England's greatest living artist'. More accurate than both of these, *The Guardian* described him as an 'anti-Morrissey', 'the alternative Neil Tennant' and 'the new Ivor Cutler'.

Momus found a distinctive niche for his leftfield and outsider music, first in the late 1980s and early 1990s on Creation Records with albums such as *Tender Pervert* (1988) and *Hippopotamomus* (1991), and then on Cherry Red Records with such classics as *Slender Sherbert* (1995), *The Little Red Songbook* (1998) and *Stars Forever* (1999).

These collections were in many respects years ahead of their time. Yes there is some similarity with Morrissey before it all went wrong: the arch-wit, the constant observation of life from the perspective of the outsider, and the championing of those who are usually overlooked. But the differences were always as important.

Whereas Morrissey sadly for us as well as him, took himself too seriously, with Momus there has always been an ambiguity, playfulness, and exploration of what is authentic and inauthentic. The voice and perspective of Momus has never been monochromatic and static, but always on the move, surprising, provoking and unsettling. In this, he clearly draws from Bowie, art school, punk and new wave, but also from Serge Gainsbourg, while preparing the ground for a host of mid-1990s alt-pop acts such as Belle and Sebastian, Pulp and The Divine Comedy.

There was anti-pop stardom in his take on the world yearning for pop fame in such classics as 'I Was a Maoist Intellectual' about being a revolutionary in the music industry which contains the great signing off line: 'My downfall came from being the three things the working class hated: Agitated, organised and over-educated.' At the same time there was 'Love on Ice', his view of Torvill and Dean as gay icons and martyrs. There is the sheer genius of *Stars Forever* where Momus, facing a potentially ruinous law suit, put together a double album with thirty patrons each paying $1,000 to have a song written about their lives. It is an act of survival, which raises big questions about the relationship of art and commerce, while looking into the horrid heart of the coming celebrity culture that now threatens to infect all public life.

Despite this prolific and rich back catalogue *The Book of Scotlands* came at first as a surprise, emerging from a purple patch which also saw Momus pen his first ever novel, *The Book of Jokes*. In the pages within we enter over 150 parallel Scotlands of past, present and future, of parallel universes and alternative worlds. This breathtaking mixture of the serious, surreal, unreal, magical and macabre displays ideas, confidence and daringness that deserve to be recognised, applauded and most of all, enjoyed.

There are so many joyful, thought provoking and challenging Scotlands within the pages, some just one or two lines, and many extended essays and reflections, all of which repay visiting and revisiting. I have known and grown to love so many of these entries that drawing out a couple is near impossible.

There is the 'Scotland 45' where sexologist Alfred Kinsey and folk music archivist Alan Lomax tour the Scotland of the 1950s together and study the sex habits of the Scottish fiddler. In the 'Scotland 24' a huge black swan comes to lie in Scotland over Ayrshire and becomes part of the mythology of the nation and 'the official symbol of Scotland'. 'Everybody loved the black swan' writes Momus, and because of this: 'In films and songs and books it was portrayed as a lucky charm, a saviour, a mascot'. It became part of our identity, how we saw ourselves, boosting tourism and national pride, and then it left, flying away to New Zealand, leaving people bereft and missing something they once thought a constant.

'Scotland 166' states, in what might be a credo for the book, 'The Scotland in which four hundred years of influence from Calvin is replaced by four hundred years of profound influence from Calvino.' 'Scotland 76' reveals the ongoing influence of Bowie: 'The mist-filled Scotland in which people chant Hugh MacDiarmid poems over Side Two of David Bowie's *Low*'. But while the last two examples show Momus wearing his own heart literally on his sleeve, most of the book takes the course of being mischievous and even gently subversive. The country of 'Scotland 144' takes a swipe at our attempt to invent our own homegrown pseudo-puritanism and fundamentalism of the present, under the leadership of Brent Shouter. Brent is described as 'Scotland's moral puppeteer' – clearly inspired by Brian Souter – and his campaign doesn't end the way he thought it might, for himself or the country.

The imagination and intelligence that Momus invokes in these pages has some commonalities with such Scottish rare talents as Ivor Cutler, Alasdair Gray, Bill Duncan (and his *The Wee Book of Calvin* in particular) and Michael Marra. Perhaps in our country this is still a male only eccentricness, but hopefully this is at last beginning to change, and Momus in a small way has offered an alternative version of maleness, gender and sexual identity. Even more, in his outsider metaphysical humour and psychosexual intelligence, he is clearly in a field all of his own.

There are so many wonderful things about this book. The fact that it exists is one, and that it is championed by a Scottish publisher to reach the audience it deserves is cause for celebration. There is also the Scotland that is self-consciously missing from this book. There isn't an invocation of a workerist, Red Clydeside, or statist Scotland anywhere. There is no articulation of a single story as our mobilising myth, nor is there much in the way of formal politics. Margaret Thatcher – in what must be a first – does not make an appearance, as saint or sinner. Nor does Alex Salmond. But then again neither does football.

This strange world offers a welcome departure from the earnest scripts of the dominant discourses of recent decades in the book version of Scotland: the male moral certainties of the William McIlvanneys and James Kelmans and their equivalents who have had their place and given us so much, but have become an official alternative account of the country.

Reflecting on *The Book of Scotlands* and the joyful range of insights and surprises that are contained on these pages says something about where Scotland now sits in the lull – after the Big Bang of the indyref and the wreckage of Brexit. The imagination, intelligence and daringness on display are exactly the creative and collective characteristics we need to show as a nation and society.

Now more than ever we need to jump into different imaginations, and to provoke, play and see from different directions and perspectives our country and the world. That requires having no boundaries or no-go areas about what and how we imagine, articulate and create (beyond issues of decency, discrimination and bigotry). We should not be leaving any stones or traditions unturned and in this *The Book of Scotlands* is both an inspiration and in its own way a guide on how to be a provocateur. Thank you Momus for this and everything.

Preface

The Book of Scotlands was written in 2009, when I was living in Berlin. Commissioned by the German writer Ingo Niermann for his Sternberg series Solutions, it was somewhat modelled on his influential book about Germany, Umbauland, which translates as 'construction site nation' or, literally, 'reconstruction land'. One of Ingo's ten provocative visions for a future Germany was that a new German grammar should be devised, somewhere between Orwell's Newspeak and the radically streamlined French introduced after the 1789 revolution. This was Rededeutsch, originally pitched as a satirical design project by Redesigndeutschland (Niermann and puckish Berlin designer Rafael Horzon), and first described in Ingo's column in the Berlin electronic culture magazine *DeBug*.

The Book of Scotlands was my second book (the first was a scurrilous novel, *The Book of Jokes*, published by Dalkey Archive Press in Chicago). In retrospect, I see it coming very much out of a certain ferment happening in Berlin in the first decade of the 21st century. Sternberg is an art publisher, and these visions of Scotland are an offshoot of Berlin's art scene: the lectures and salons that took place in Horzon's studio in Mitte, the playful curation at the Haus der Kulturen der Welt, the satirical design commentary of *DeBug*, the radical philosophy published by the Merve imprint.

When Caroline Schneider at Sternberg asked Niermann to expand Umbauland into a series of books about various nations, he contacted me – I'd already covered his activities for *Design Observer* and my blog, *Click Opera* – and suggested I write one ('or even two') books for the series. And in fact after the book about Scotland I went on to write *The Book of Japans* (2011), which also has a parallel Scotland as its backdrop: a group of Shetland shepherds who claim to have time-travelled to the future of Japan are grilled by a panel of experts, intrigued by the fact that these 'idiots' have correctly predicted the date of a major earthquake.

If it sounds odd that Berlin should be the hub of this thinktanking about the future of Scotland, it's worth remembering the role Germany played in the concoction (largely thanks to Sir Walter Scott) of Scotland's current identity – Goethe and those who followed him would be drawn, from the era of early Romanticism well into the 19th century, to an image of Scotland they'd encountered in the Ossian poems of James Macpherson, the bucolic-apocalyptic fiction of James Hogg, or Mendelssohn's music invoking Fingal's Cave and a largely imaginary Hebrides.

Keenly aware that there was an independence debate raging in my homeland, I wanted to ensure that the 'wooden tongue' of official discourse wasn't the only form the national dialogue should take: something delirious and speculative was also necessary, a sort of brainstorming session about possible future Scotlands which would emphasise our nation's protean elasticity. An influential precursor was the anthology *Without Day*, compiled by the poet Alec Finlay and published by Pocketbooks in 2001. Finlay asked a hundred Scottish writers and artists to celebrate the arrival of the devolved Scottish parliament by making proposals for artworks, performances and other interventions informed by the promise made in 1707, at the closure of the original Scottish parliament, that it would reconvene at some unspecified future date (hence *sine die* or 'without day'). Other important influences were Brian Eno's ideas about 'possible musics' from an imaginary 'fourth world', or David Bowie's line that art is a safe space for dangerous speculations, a zone in which 'you can crash the plane and walk away'.

Designer Zak Kyes, concocting the cover for the Sternberg edition of *The Book of Scotlands*, reversed the colour of the Scottish flag, rotated it, and chose from the text a slogan to emblazon across it: 'Every lie creates a parallel world. The world in which it is true.'

We often talk negatively about lies in politics, but what we forget is that lies can be productive, generative: they're proposals for conditions that do not currently exist, but might. A lie can be an intention, a toe in the water, a feasibility study, a design blueprint, a piece of speculative fiction, a fervent wish or a feverish dream. I chose to lie about Scotland because I love my land – as much for what it may become as what it is, as much a place to dream about as to know.

Nick Currie (Momus)
Berlin 2018

SCOTLAND 55

There are ten major cities in Scotland, named for the rivers they stand on:

Clydopolis
Forthopolis
Donopolis
Tayopolis
Speyopolis
Deepolis
Tweedopolis
Nithopolis
Deveropolis
Annanopolis

These ten cities are arranged in a strict circle, as in a decimal clockface, around Scotland's striking central feature: an enormous, perfectly circular volcano rising ten thousand metres above sea level. The volcano is called Mount Death.

There is no point in Scotland from which Mount Death cannot be seen, but its bulk hides each city from all the others. The rim of the volcano's crater is always white with snow, and steam constantly rises from the circular lake within.

Each city has built roads up the curved sides of the volcano to Deathhorn, the intense resort situated on the cliff of the crater's inner edge. Here, glass-walled hotels, casinos, nightclubs and leisure complexes throw a blaze of golden electric light into the hot fog of the central loch, which bubbles perpetually, releasing clouds of steam which turn quickly into thunderstorms.

Up here, the air is thin and revellers wear gas masks fitted with oxygen tanks. The masks also protect tourists from the foul odour. Nevertheless, some hotels incorporate chutes which deposit their boldest guests, naked, into the hot dark seismic swell below. A short swim is considered salutary for the health. A long swim will result in certain death.

There's nothing like a quick trip to Deathhorn to rekindle guttering *joie de vivre*. Uncertain whether they'll come back to the ten cities alive, Scots experience ten times the intensity up at the resort as they do in the world below. Time in Deathhorn seems to pass ten times more quickly, and each event feels ten times more precious.

The volcano straddles the active Findhorn Fault. As a result, the loch is constantly erupting, sending great plumes of scalding lava crashing against this or that part of the cliff resort of Deathhorn. Broken buildings must constantly be repaired by orange cranes, and the corpses of the many casualties are thrown into the circular loch in ceremonies led by purple-clad priests of the ancient Horn religion, men who live in vertiginous monasteries interspersed with the hotels.

Every hundred years, more or less exactly, the volcano explodes in a massive eruption, spilling over its rims and burying one of the ten cities in lava, killing everyone living there. Although the timing of these eruptions can be calculated, the direction of the lava flow depends on various factors which can't be. No evacuations are made; every Scot knows there is just a 10% chance that his city will be the unfortunate one.

Preserved in lava as in aspic, the stricken city becomes a museum of Scottish life for the following century, a monument to the customs of its time much visited by grateful survivors from the other nine.

When one hundred years have passed, the museum-city is excavated and redeveloped, and Mount Death duly engulfs another city in lava. So far, the equitable mountain has never buried the same city twice.

SCOTLAND 19

The Scotland which – nobody disagrees! – boasts the world's most beautiful women, by far.

SCOTLAND 54

The Scotland in which you can hear a pin drop. There used to be a clock hung up at the end of it, but the ticking drove us all mad.

SCOTLAND 46

Lerwick is a cluster of thatched shacks built on slabs of komatiite rock, overlooking the windswept Iapetus Ocean. When my mother and I arrive, the harbour is filled with the longships of Harald Fairhair, king of Norway, and thronged by the Viking descendants of Earl Rognvald. When these fearsome men come ashore they take what they want, shouting orders in Norn, a language descended from Old Norse by way of Faroese and Icelandic.

We're warned against the Vikings by a man named Thord 'Dragon Skull'. He's threshing oats from the straw in a barn. He also advises us to beware of Nyuggles, the ghostly horses lurking round streams and lochs. They seem docile, he says, but should the weary traveller dare to mount one, a Nyuggle will instantly bolt for the nearest body of water, drowning its rider. There are also risks associated with boat travel in these parts; sea serpents known as Brigdi entwine the gunwales of vessels with finny tentacles, then dive to the depths, dragging craft and passengers with them.

We thank Thord 'Dragon Skull' for his advice, refusing his kind offer of plated piltocks (the staple here, a sort of prehistoric fish) and cabbage. We pass a group of children begging in costumes of straw. 'Skeklers,' explains a young lady, who dashes off because she's chasing a crow to her future husband's house.

We had hoped to see Lerwick's fire festival, in which young men drag burning tar barrels through the streets and finally haul a longship up a hill, but, annoyed by the destruction of their vessels, the Vikings have banned the ceremony.

We come upon a circle of islanders singing veeseks – long-versed ballads recited from memory and accompanied by clapping. They break into a song that goes 'balloo ballili, balloo ballili, balloo baa'.

Between Beltin Day, when haaf fishing begins, and Johnsmas, when it ends, bonfires are set on hilltops to ward off witches unpropitious to the catch. The fishermen drink toasts and the young folk eat a special gruel. This is a season favoured by Finns, spirits which can change their shape at will.

At nine o'clock in the evening, we're lucky enough to witness the earnest fiddle dance of the six tall Geysers, in a sandy-floored room filled with giggling Brides Maidens. First, the best man announces there's enough whisky and meat for all comers. Then the fiddler begins to scrape out the Geyser's Spring, and the tall grave Scuddler ambles in, his face swathed in bandages, head and body wrapped in garments – the principal of which is a sheathed petticoat of gloy straw tied with ribbons which dangle from him in every hue, trailing the earth of the dim hall.

The Scuddler snorts like a mare, paws the ground, and dances in a slow, grotesque manner to the music of the fiddle. Soon he is joined by The Gentleman, and then by The Fool, and so on, until all six Geysers are present, solemnly dancing. None speaks, for their identities must be kept secret from the Brides Maidens.

As they dance, I'm lost in thought. In how many of, say, a thousand parallel worlds in which the people of the past are offered a choice between their life and ours, do they choose their own? How much of what we now consider beauty – the muted colours of a croft's workspaces below its thatched roof, the pancreatic forms of the paleolithic brochs and roundhouses we've visited – would be traded in a flash by these 'virtuous poor' for my mother's Citroën and its longboat shaped digital speedometer display?

But the Bronze Age people I bring back with me to the Citroën turn away at the last minute, shaking their heads and proclaiming that the future is not the place for them.

They will return to their mossy warrens, they tell me, mostly in sign language. They love their familiar brochs, their cold rock flagstones, their thatched warrens standing on drystone foundations, constantly battered by the wind.

I walk back to the car, where my mother sits listening to the shipping forecast.

SCOTLAND 112

The newscasters on STV News get dirtier and dirtier every time I see them. I mean *literally*.

At first it was just an odd dusty patch here or there, the kind of thing you might put down to a flare on the lens or perspiration under bright studio lights. Just the light smudging of foundation powder on a dark collar.

But then unmistakable stains appeared; food stains, sperm stains, urine.

'Can't they afford a dry cleaner?' people asked. 'These dirty newscasters are letting Scotland down!'

You'd be watching the news, and you'd feel like you could smell it. Soon it became a news story in its own right. Wearing a cream-coloured suit with moth-eaten lapels and a shit-smeared pink cravat, anchor Jim Beamie announced it like this:

'The STV News team has been called upon to justify the self-presentation standards of its newscasters. Here is a statement from executive producer Brian McNaughton-Naughtie.'

McNaughton-Naughtie was dressed in rags incandescent with putrefaction. Clouds of smoke rose continually from his body, which bubbled like a cauldron of stink. You could hear the studio technicians choking as he prepared to speak.

'The dirty appearance of the STV presenters,' he announced, 'far from being something accidental, was a deliberate editorial policy on my part. I will try to explain my motivations. The news is not a pleasant thing – in fact, it's a succession of some of the world's least pleasant things, one after the other. Wars, rapes, accidents, deaths, atrocities, misfortunes of all sorts.'

There was a minor explosion on McNaughton-Naughtie's head as a boil burst, spattering the lens of the camera with something yellowish green.

'One problem faced by all news anchors is tone. Just what sort of manner do you adopt when describing a plane heavy with 156 'souls', which aborts take-off and ploughs into a school, killing 74 children? You can look grave, but is that enough, when, by the end of the programme, you make light-hearted remarks about the alpaca twins born at the zoo?'

'I mean, life goes on, of course. But should it?'

One of McNaughton-Naughtie's arms fell off and was quickly swarmed by a seething mass of bobbing, weaving maggots.

'In light of this, I made a decision,' Naughtie continued, his broken head lolling and leering on his shoulder, an orange fluid spilling from his ear. 'I decided to employ what T.S. Eliot called an 'objective correlative' to the tragedies of the news. Even the word 'tragedy' is limp and anaemic, a shorthand insufficient to the things it describes.'

McNaughton-Naughtie's neck seemed to sag. A technician ran up from behind, crouched just out of sight of the camera, and held up his head.

'In seeking to make the atrocities of the Scottish news visible to my viewers, I settled on certain effects of putrefaction. Nothing less could communicate the full horror of the events we cover, for only putrefaction has an immediate, visceral effect. Even if you can't smell the rotting matter in this studio, you can imagine it.'

McNaughton-Naughtie's face was melting, revealing a skull already wriggling with micro-organisms.

'I achieved the effects I did,' he continued, his body alive with flies, 'by injecting tiny vermin of all sorts beneath my own skin and the skins of my employees. It is a measure of their dedication to the job – a 24/7 commitment – that they agreed, and complied, at considerable cost to themselves and their personal relationships.'

'We would also like to thank you, the audience, for persisting with us despite our increasingly disgusting visual condition, and indeed, for viewing in ever increasing numbers.'

McNaughton-Naughtie's head fell off completely, though it continued speaking faintly from somewhere down on the floor. No words could be distinguished, but a puddle of golden liquid – not quite syrup, not quite shit – seeped across the desktop and began to drip to the floor with a tip, tip, tip.

'And now for the rest of this evening's news,' smiled Jim Beamie. 'At Glasgow Zoo, good things come in twos. This morning, one of the alpacas gave birth to twins.'

SCOTLAND 23

The Scotland in which everything is coloured Pantone 1655. Everything not coloured Pantone 1655 is destroyed by fire in a 'colour heap'.

SCOTLAND 164

The Scotland in which four hundred years of profound influence from Calvin is replaced by four hundred years of profound influence from Calvino.

SCOTLAND 78

The Scotland in which all maps of the country are displayed upside-down and back-to-front to make everything fresh.

SCOTLAND 45

It's a little-known fact that Alfred Kinsey came to Scotland shortly after publishing *Sexual Behavior in the Human Female*. He came with his friend Alan Lomax, the ethno-musicologist. It was partly a holiday, but the pair also wanted to pursue their interests; Lomax wanted to make recordings of sea shanties, Kinsey to compile data on Scottish masturbation.

And so, over three weeks during the hot summer of 1954, the two Americans travelled the length and breadth of Scotland. They listened to old sailors singing what they remembered of sea songs, and harvested sensitive data on masturbation. No sooner had an old man put down his fiddle after playing for Lomax's Revox than he was quizzed by Kinsey on his one-handed technique. The pike-faced old musicians were assured that, although all credit would be given them for the music, for the sex survey they would be strictly Trad/Anon.

Lomax managed to record some wonderful ballads, but what Kinsey discovered shocked him profoundly. Scots were masturbating far too much; on average, 6.7 times per day. At this rate of sexual squandor, the nation wouldn't last far beyond 1978. Something had to be done.

Kinsey and Lomax formed a delegation and made an urgent visit to the Scottish government. Lomax handed over priceless folk recordings, then Kinsey rose to speak.

'Gentlemen,' he said, 'after an extensive random

survey of Scottish sexual habits, mostly focused on fiddlers, I have made a disturbing discovery. The Scots are masturbating too much. Birth and productivity rates are sure to nosedive over the next decades. At this rate, there won't be a single Scot left by the year 2000.'

The Scottish leaders took Kinsey seriously; after all, he had recently appeared on the cover of *Time* magazine, surrounded by birds, flowers and bees.

'What do you suggest we do?' they asked.

Kinsey outlined an extensive promotional campaign with the slogan 'Stop masturbating!'

Only this direct approach could bring the nation to its senses, and save it from sinking to its knees.

After the meeting, Kinsey and Lomax were given bowls of Scottish onion soup and glasses of Scottish mead before being driven to Turnhouse Airport and put aboard a Caravelle jet bound for New York. They sat in first class, smoking briarwood pipes and gazing down at the Atlantic through gaily curtained floor-to-ceiling windows (later deemed a serious design flaw).

The Scottish government decided to act on Kinsey's advice. They launched a major publicity campaign advising the Scottish people to 'Stop masturbating!'. Ads were shown in cinemas before and after every film (it was still the age of almost universal cinema- going). They featured a crowd of old sea dog fiddlers sawing away vigorously at violins, suddenly interrupted by Stanley Baxter. Pushing the men aside and screwing up his rough-hewn Glasgow face, Baxter said directly into the camera:

'STOP MASTURBATING!'

The campaign was a great success. Masturbation quickly went out of fashion in Scotland, and the results didn't take long to make themselves felt. Work productivity rates soared along with the birthrate, and the nation's GDP skyrocketed. Before long there was enough excess income for Scottish Prime Minister Margaret Muir to promise, in a famous 1961 speech, that Scotland would put a man on the moon before decade's end.

In 1969 the entire world watched as that promise was fulfilled on live television. I remember the scene well. I was lying in an air-conditioned room in the French city of Montpellier, masturbating.

SCOTLAND 11

The Scotland in which the most popular music venues are the windswept hillsides of Akio Suzuki's Resonant Spaces Tour: Smoo Cave, Durness; Ring of Brodgar, Orkney; Lyness Oil Tank, Hoy; Tugnet Ice House, Spey Bay; Wormit Reservoir, Fife; and the Hamilton Mausoleum.

SCOTLAND 82

The Scotland whose 'auld alliance' was with Iceland.

SCOTLAND 130

The Scotland whose capital is known fondly as 'Auld Greeky' and the Greece whose capital is 'the Edinburgh of the South'.

SCOTLAND 149

The Scotland which spent fifty years at war with Austria, perfecting its weaponry by sending spies to the Tyrolian republic.

SCOTLAND 86

During the Septonian plenum of the Eighth Scotian luminum, constitutional and financial crisis struck. Scotia had been offered a bridging package by the International Praxi-Collegiate after third quarter expenditures alone had outstripped its annual income.

The state's solar wind duck installation disaster was the major cause: the programme – intended to cover all of Scotia's energy needs – was hit hard by the Sturton-Ash asteroid shower and exceptionally inclement solar flares during early summer. Repro-animal clonage exports were also damaged by the tsetse-hacker incident. Combined with ongoing soil erosion and desertification – which had already cut Scotia's olive yields by a terce – the result was a disastrous hit to the state pocket.

Troubles never come singly. The year 2252 also saw Scotia's worst constitutional crisis in almost a unit. To explain exactly what happened, we would have to delve back into the arcana of the state's establishment in the early 21st century. Suffice it to say, back then, proportional language-based voting arrangements were put in place which led – albeit a century later – to the bitter tactical deadlocks of the 2230s, the turbo-log war of 2243, and the resulting consignment of Scotia's legal framework to sterile judgebots for an unprecedented six years.

Just when affairs seemed to have stabilised and the Global Stripe Panel issued a decree to return Scotia to human control, the sterile judgebots mounted a coup, arguing that Scotia needed to be made safe for electronic as well as human citizens. Since the sterile judgebots held the quantum data keys to Scotia's ecocalibration – not to mention sixteen of its core mechanical lemon rods – they saw more than 87% of their demands met.

Scotia consequently became an offshore identity haven for millions of electronic refugees. The resulting ghost economy almost wiped out all remaining human-oriented industries. It wasn't until the Revolution of the Black Octagon that Scotia once more had a human ward, in the shape of our current leader, Bonnie Billy Prince, that blazing architect of the Diagonal Restoration.

Long may he reign!

SCOTLAND 100

The Scotland climate change has covered in equatorial rainforests and the laboratory which produced Dolly the Sheep has stocked with as many man-made lemurs as there are presently pheasants.

SCOTLAND 119

The Scotland which models itself on the Japan of the Heian period, described by one dissenter – the Reverend James Murdoch, writing at the end of the 19th century – as 'an ever pullulating brood of greedy, needy, frivolous dilettante, as often as not foully licentious, utterly effeminate, incapable of any worthy achievement, but withal the polished exponents of high breeding and correct form'.

SCOTLAND 32

The Scotland replicated in miniature by Nova Caledonia, a biodiversity lifeship suspended in geostationary orbit 35,786 vertical kilometres above Perth.

SCOTLAND 87

The communist Scotland which renationalises all its industries and lives according to the principle 'from each according to his ability, to each according to his need'.

SCOTLAND 72

The hypercapitalist Scotland in which one thousand tiny businesses throng every street and every floor of every building, and cater to every possible human need, and never close.

SCOTLAND 116

As part of your new post in Scotland, you will be dealing with Scottish men and women on a daily basis. With a view to making these interactions as unproblematical as possible, the company has put together this *Employee's Guide to the Scots*. This is not a starry-eyed or romantic view of the Scottish people, but a realistic assessment based on known traits and issues. It is designed to facilitate a smooth flow of daily interactions, and to help you deal with trouble when it occurs.

Please bear in mind at all times that we are guests here. The Scottish government has allowed us to operate in their country, and we should conduct ourselves in a mannerly and considerate way within the context of Scotland as we find it, no matter what our personal views of the political situation may be.

Despite the prevailing view that the Scotsman is naturally lazy, you will find that many Scots are dedicated workers who fulfil all you ask of them, albeit over a slightly longer period of time, and with more grumbling and resentment than you might encounter back home.

Rumours that the Scots poison drinking water are old racist lore, long ago debunked. But you should nevertheless bear in mind that poor fertilisers and generally low standards of hygiene make caution necessary when consuming locally produced foodstuffs. Remember to boil all drinking water. There is mounting evidence, too, that you should avoid feeding your baby with Scottish milk substitutes. Breast-feed if possible, but not in public.

It is advisable to wear a face mask when walking in Scottish urban environments. Lax environmental standards and the endemic corruption which unfortunately prevails at all levels of Scottish government have led to severely degraded air quality, making asthma and other serious respiratory illnesses almost universal here.

You should also take care to guard your personal possessions and remain vigilant in public places at all times. Even the poorest of us is richer than the average Scot by a factor of ten; we therefore present a juicy target for thieves and brigands. Of course, the punishment for robbing us is severe – in most cases, the culprit will be summarily executed by government militia. It's worth bearing in mind, though, that human life is held in lower regard here than it is in our own nation. A family with ten children, barely living at subsistence level, will think nothing of sending adolescent males to take risks which might easily result in their deaths. After all, there is always another Scot where he came from.

As you are doubtless aware if you read the newspapers, there are agitators and extremists at the fringes of Scottish society who will think nothing of strapping explosives to their children's chests and sending them to our factories, our canteens, our embassies, our installations. Even though these children, with their big green eyes and tufty ginger hair, might seem appealing as they approach with a smile, remember that it may well be a trap. If in doubt, use your company-supplied weapon and, following your range training, shoot to kill.

Most of the Scots you encounter in your daily working life, however, will be civilised and considerate individuals, eager to earn much needed cash and wary of the extremists in their midst who whisper malicious lies about us and our presence in their land. You might serve the entire period of your post without witnessing a single explosion, or even once being kidnapped, taken to caves in the mountains, and tortured.

Your daily life in Scotland will hopefully be uneventful, disturbed, if at all, by small inconveniences: the undeniably brash rudeness of the Scots, the backward sexist way in which they treat their womenfolk, their protests outside our facilities, motivated by objections to our equal treatment of their women and what they see as the lax, sexually provocative dress codes we enforce on them.

Poor hygiene, endless outbreaks of infectious disease, and insect borne blights and plagues will undoubtedly dog your stay, but if you minimise contact with the natives – especially sexual contact – all should be well. And do undergo the whole range of preventive injections the company offers.

Although at first you will find the Scots difficult to tell apart – coarse ginger hair and poor quality, spotty skin predominate – by the end of your stay you will certainly know a few by name, and may have developed feelings of affection for them. In a precious few you will even discover hidden qualities of loyalty, selflessness and gratitude.

Expect to be cheated in your daily shopping expeditions, but remember prices are so cheap here that you will end up saving on your expenditures even with all the rip-offs factored in.

You should avoid any business dealings with the Scottish mafia, who control much of the nation's grey economy, especially the organised begging (never donate!) and the night markets, full of copyright-infringing faked and forged goods. Scottish-made toys often include lead paint, by the way, so if you have children, import their toys from abroad.

If anyone demands protection money, show your embossed company ID card and they should be deterred by our well-known, no-nonsense policy of deadly retaliation. Be aware, however, that triad influence extends all the way to the top of the Scottish government. Leave it to us to deal with that.

As a general cultural rule of thumb, remember that today's Scots are living in something very much like our own 14th century. Rights we take for granted are still, for them, far in the future. In many ways, they aren't yet ready for them. For this reason, it's worth pausing before condemning the current Scottish military dictatorship as 'fascist' or decrying its admittedly appalling human rights record. Democracy, basic rights and the rule of law are luxuries which Scotland may one day enjoy, thanks to the opportunities for economic development that companies like ours are affording it. But this will take time.

You will certainly find the customs of the Scots – their ribald fire festivals, for instance – superstitious, and their religion harsh and unforgiving. But remember that this is a cunning and resourceful people, a people which has, somehow, invented many of the key technologies of modern life – the steam engine, the telephone, the television – even if they didn't long retain control of them. They also enjoy surprising longevity; your family retainer may still be serving your sons, and the sons of your sons.

You will recoil in horror from the ideology of Scottish zealots who, with ever increasing stridency, advocate the implementation of Scottish customs, Scottish dress and religious-based Scottish law even beyond the borders of Scotland. Although they lack the fire power to achieve this militarily, many believe that a demographic time bomb will spread their values across a widening area, simply because the Scots are reproducing faster than we are.

Nevertheless, we have the upper hand for the moment. We are the strong ones, and the rich ones. We have the technology, the money and the IQ levels to maintain our dominance. Deep down, the Scots know this and respect us for it. Strength, after all, is what they value above all things.

A few employees are inclined to feel sympathy for the Scots, for their poverty, their rich folk culture, their resilience, their struggle for autonomy. After a few years in Scotland, some of these well-intentioned individuals even begin baptising their children, circumcising their wives, dressing in tartan, studying Calvinism, practising Celtic natural healing, observing the curfew and learning the fiddle.

We warn very strongly against making concessions of this type. When we see sympathies like these developing – no matter how well-intentioned – it is our corporate policy to send the employees concerned to other, more demanding posts at the furthest reaches of the Empire.

SCOTLAND 122

The Scotland in which Lord Summerisle's human sacrifice does indeed bring a full and florid harvest the following year.

SCOTLAND 163

The Scotland in which the national dish is skewered raw horse meat flavoured with ginger and coriander.

SCOTLAND 134

The Scotland in which controlled nuclear explosions along the Highland Boundary Fault release a burst of seismic energy sufficient to flatten the entire country and transform it into a car park for England.

SCOTLAND 162

King Mackie the Mack was cursed by the birth of a blind son, whom he christened Raymond the Blind.

Gathering his courtiers and wise men around him, King Mackie asked their advice.

'Scotland cannot be led by a blind man,' he said. 'And yet the royal line must pass through my loins. What is to be done?'

The men told him the most obvious solution: Mackie must produce other children with his wife, Queen Sirloin. When a suitable boy was born, the laws of succession would be amended and the throne would pass, in due course, to the younger son in place of the elder.

The lords of law determined that this was constitutionally possible, and Mackie retired to his royal sleeping chamber with Sirloin to carry out the plan.

Soon she was pregnant again. But – to the horror of the royal court and the whole of Scotland – the next child, again a son, was also blind.

'This is a disaster!' Mackie exclaimed when the doctors told him the news. 'We are cursed!'

But his courtiers told him not to be discouraged, and to try again. So once more Mackie retired to the bedchamber with Sirloin. The queen became pregnant again, and again the child – a boy – was blind.

'I have affronted the gods,' said King Mackie. 'They are angry with me, and clearly I must placate them.'

And so Mackie swore to spend twelve years in exile, wandering Scotland dressed in rags. Only by this extreme act of expiation would he persuade the gods of his sincerity.

Mackie left the royal castle early one morning, dressed as a beggar. No one accompanied him, but Queen Sirloin waved a tearful farewell from the lockhouse overlooking the ramparts.

During his twelve years of exile, Mackie had many adventures. He earned his living first as a candlemaker, later as a crow-catcher, still later as a seer.

He became lonely and settled down in Dunbar with a beautiful washerwoman, though he was careful never to consummate the relationship. When Maggie (that was the name of the beautiful washerwoman) asked why he held back from physical intimacy, Mackie explained that he couldn't forget an old flame. Little did Maggie suspect that this old love was, in fact, the queen.

When eleven years and eleven months had passed, Mackie began to make his way back towards the castle. Much had changed during the years of his exile. The whole structure of the castle was different. Strange skeletal forms cluttered the esplanade, complicated iron gantries surmounted by bright spots of fire. Iron horses cantered about noiselessly, and iron birds flew through the air, making a sound like thunder.

Mackie tried to explain to himself how these changes had come about.

'A new king has taken over Scotland,' he exclaimed. 'I will confront the usurper and demand that my throne be returned. Then I will be reunited with my beloved Queen Sirloin, and we shall produce a sighted son.'

So the king strode up to his castle. A couple of fools tried to bar his way, jingling purses full of coins and shouting 'Ticket, sir, ticket!' But the king ignored them and dashed across the drawbridge.

At first it was hard for Mackie to get his bearings atop the castle rock. All sorts of strange new buildings stood where once there had been open space.

When he reached the only building he recognised – St Margaret's Chapel – the king was astounded by the view over the turrets. His capital city had expanded to ten or twenty times its previous size! Apart from the physical features of the landscape – the slope of the Royal Mile, the red stone curtain of Salisbury Crags, the range of the

Pentlands on the horizon, the Firth of Forth and the hills of Fife – everything had changed.

'What has become of my kingdom?' he cried. But the people around Mackie paid no attention. They were busy looking at each other with clicking metal eyes. And talking, on hand-held metal boxes, to themselves.

'Yeah,' said one man, dressed in a curious species of soft chain mail, 'we'll be there at two – want to catch the Whisky Heritage Centre and the Camera Obscura after this.'

Mackie strode up to the man. 'What are you doing in my castle?' he demanded. 'And where is my wife, Queen Sirloin?' He knocked the metal box from the man's hand to the cobbled ground.

'Hey, that's my phone!' shouted the man.

'Where is Queen Sirloin?' repeated the king. 'And who is in charge of this place? I am King Mackie the Mack, rightful king of Scotland, and I have returned after twelve years of exile.'

'Listen, mate,' said the tourist, 'I don't care if you're Jesus-fucking-Christ, you can't just toss people's mobiles around like that. I'm going to have to report you.'

And he strode quickly off.

The king stumbled around in confusion, looking for the entrance to his private chambers. But the building seemed to have vanished. As he hammered on the door of a newer, much bigger building standing in its place, two men dressed in oddly coloured tartans came up to him.

'We understand you've been creating a disturbance, sir,'

they said. 'Can you tell us what happened just now?'

'Are you liege lords to His Majesty the King of Scotland?' roared Mackie. 'Then you should fall at my feet and pay me your most reverent respects. For I am your king, returned from twelve years of exile.'

One of the men stepped forward, about to grab Mack by the shoulder, but the other restrained him. 'Jim,' he hissed, 'Jim, what he's saying is right. I recognise him from the painting in the library – the one hanging above the fireplace. It *is* King Mackie the Mack, back after twelve hundred years.'

And both men fell to their knees.

'Twelve hundred years?' demanded Mackie. 'Have I really been away that long? It was only supposed to be twelve!'

That afternoon the men took Mackie to a room lined with the most valuable precious metals, a room which had been kept in readiness for him for twelve hundred years. Mackie was bathed and clothed in ermines.

A meeting of all the chief authorities of Scotland was called, and one by one they paid their respects to the king, marvelling that he had returned after so long. One by one, Mackie gave the men his blessing and thanked them for their faithfulness during his exile.

Over the next few weeks, the king was tutored in all of the changes that had taken place over the last twelve hundred years. He was instructed in the rudiments of technological development, the constitution, modern history, warfare, transport, and statecraft.

Finally, with great fanfare, the king was reinstated as chief executive and monarch of Scotland. The world's media was ablaze with the news, trumpeting: 'RETURN OF KING MACKIE THE MACK!' and 'THE MACK IS BACK!'

Mackie proved a fair and a just king, and under his renewed authority Scotland flourished. With his knowledge of harsher, simpler times and his strong expectations of loyalty, he was able to bring an unprecedented unity and sense of purpose to the nation. But he wasn't stuck in the past; King Mackie wholeheartedly embraced renewable energy sources, implementing, for instance, widescale wind and wave energy harvesting programmes along Scotland's gusty coasts and across her rolling uplands. He also achieved impressive levels of reforestation.

The king's great disappointment, though, was that he never saw his beloved Sirloin again. Waiting in vain for him, she had perished in the year 822.

SCOTLAND 30

The Scotland in which the administrative capital is moved to Inversneckie, the city founded by vaudevillian Harry Gordon.

SCOTLAND 36

The Scotland in which Scottish Christians are devoured daily by Scottish lions at McCaig's Folly, the Scottish amphitheatre atop the hill overlooking that 'gateway to the Isles', Oban.

SCOTLAND 101

Scotland begins as soon as you board a Scottish plane. For me, this time, it begins when I board ScotiaAir's flight 7788 at Kansai International airport.

A twelve hour flight gives me lots of time to observe the ScotiaAir hostesses. My flight is full of Scottish people returning from package and shopping holidays in Japan (few Japanese go to Scotland as tourists), so there's a sense that the hostesses are authority figures for fellow Scots, rather than ambassadors of Scottish culture for foreign tourists.

They represent authority in the typical way domestic Scottish service workers do: they're solicitous, formal, fragrant, theatrical, robotic, considerate, authoritative and yet fawning. Their 'submission' to the passengers is a kind of pantomime act concealing their power over us.

Different attendants have different styles; an older woman has a wheedlingly generous maternal manner, speaking to us loudly and indulgently as if we were spoilt children. Another, an extremely beautiful yet frosty cold young woman with an elaborately pinned hairstyle, is slightly sarcastic in the ritualised movements with which she caters to our whims. Her compliance seems to conceal the austere glacial sexual pride of a powerful princess or witch.

I pay attention to the images in the safety film which tell me it's inconsiderate to other passengers to get drunk, or talk on a mobile phone, or listen to music on headphones. The cartoons illustrating this show nearby passengers with grey clouds over their heads, and the selfish individuals look like criminals — vandals of Scotland's gently luxurious, monumentally discreet social fabric. Selfishness criminals!

Now it all comes back to me in a rush: the super-legitimacy, the conservatism mixed with sensuality, the tight organisation, the breezy feel, the sense that something is worth more than money.

The hostesses control us with food, temperature and light. Food is, of course, Scotland's national obsession, along with sex and nature. You still sense the presence, in this culture, of an ancient fertility religion. Even here on this plane.

Prestwick International could almost be a communist airport; somewhere in North Korea, perhaps. Everywhere there's consideration as a marker of social virtue, and a pervasive horizontality. Be a good citizen! Help others! The overstaffing, the subsidy, the civic-mindedness, all suggest the kind of protected, collectivist capitalism one Scottish philosopher has called 'communist capitalism'.

I had half expected my luggage to get lost, but not only has it arrived in Scotland with me, the ScotiaAir staff are my personal guardian angels.

I can't help smiling; in the big empty hall of Terminal 1 there are fourteen ScotiaAir girls where other national airlines would employ two or three. I'm served by a blushing young trainee who bows and begs my pardon every few seconds. When I walk off looking slightly confused about where to pick up my baggage, a 'guardian angel' runs after me just to make sure I know where to go.

On the walls hang, instead of advertisements, stunningly beautiful natural scenes, backlit with fluorescence; a gully filled with blossoming trees, a dragonfly, an old wooden barn, pagan-corporate greenery. 'Welcome to Summerisle', the florid images say.

Scotland is a soft country. There's something breezy and floral about this Atlantic atoll. Sometimes you get wafts of Gulf Stream ease, a slow-paced sensuality. And yet Scotland is an incredibly efficient and uptight 'Northern' country. Imagine how Germany must seem to Africans; Scotland feels like that after you've been away for a while. It has all the ugly industrial infrastructure you see in any advanced, wealthy country, but somehow it's exaggeratedly tidy, neat, well-organised, superlegitimate.

Some adorably cute kids, a boy and a girl, are slithering by on steel rollbars, pointing at the rain flecking the airport window. Their mother indulges them for a while, then calls them to her kindly. They respond with a loud 'Aye!', an obedience which is at once utter compliance and utter delight.

Trained, in my years abroad, to question and resist and sullenly defy, I feel sheepishly rebellious in my grey t-shirt marked, in big white letters, with the words 'NON NEIN NO'. It's as if NON NEIN and NO are what my culture has trained me to say. Saying NON NEIN and NO makes me feel big and clever. 'I'm spiky, I take shit

from no one! I'm the boss, I'll sue your ass!' But when
I see how charmingly they say AYE here in Scotland,
I feel suddenly very small, silly, white and grey, like the
selfishness criminal using a mobile phone, listening to loud
music on headphones, or getting drunk and doing a stupid
dance in the aisle.

From the nocturnal shuttle bus I glimpse a corner of
a car park, pristine clean, in which a uniformed official
stands forlornly by an area marked with black and white
diagonal stripes. His job is to guide cars around this
striped area (marked with bollards striped in the same
way), but there are no cars. He wears white gloves, of
course, like the bus driver and like the officials who help
load suitcases at each stop. These bus stewards have to
make a theatrical announcement before boarding the
bus and bowing. They make this speech in the vicinity
of the bus stop even when there are no passengers at all.
After they've boarded and greeted the passengers with a
small speech and a low bow, they get off and resume their
solitary wait for the next bus.

Meanwhile, on the bus, a tape plays. It's the corporate
welcome tape of the bus company. Impossibly melancholy
and beautiful pentatonic Celtic music plays, followed
by a welcome in a female actor's voice (clipped, precise,
slightly distant and otherworldly, as if emanating from
an even-more-extremely conservative 1950s). Then the
bus driver speaks into his microphone, a husky mumble
of solicitation. I'm overwhelmed with an impression of
overlapping luxuries; the luxury of overstaffing, the luxury

of multiple audio systems, an Atlantic fertility luxury, the luxury of the utter cleanliness of everything I see and touch, the luxury of ultra-efficiency.

I am already bowing and smiling to everyone as they bow and smile to me. I feel suddenly more tender, considerate, compassionate. Glasgow slips by outside the bus. Its high density housing and elevated expressways might, in another urban context, represent hell (the blocks of flats look like oil refineries). But here, because of the refinement and tenderness of everything, they're fine. There's a soft, sensual, consensual, luxurious magic that prevails in Scotland, taking the sharpest and ugliest edges off the urban infrastructure. The Scots have the same machinery as everyone else, but they operate it more cleanly, with different cultural software, wearing white gloves. It changes everything.

Now, at home in Edinburgh, the only sounds I can hear are the gentle chunder of the Scotsonic airconditioning unit (a discreet breeze different from the harsh rush I'm used to) and some tinkling music coming from the street outside. It's the refined, sentimental, familiar melody played by the dustbin lorry.

SCOTLAND 117

The Scotland millions of Canadians, Americans, Australians and New Zealanders sail toward annually in the hope of finding a better life. Many perish in the attempt.

SCOTLAND 84

The Scotland in which the crofters evict the landlords.

SCOTLAND 26

Where is the collaboration between Ivor Cutler and Ian Hamilton Finlay? The dim Scotch sitting room during Brumaire?

SCOTLAND 71

The Scotland in which – everything in stages! – the whole concept of money is abolished, and then the euro is adopted.

SCOTLAND 98

The Scotland which makes ten or more children per family compulsory.

SCOTLAND 109

You approach this Scotland in a tour van containing the members of Sonic Flower Groove. They've just made their major label debut, and you've just finished a singer-songwriter album released by an indie label. You're all Germans, of course, and this is your first visit to Scotland. It's 1987.

As you approach the capital city via the long, straight motorway corridor, your head is full of 'the structuring myths of Scotland'. Which should you pick, the nation's notorious fascist period or the experimental cool of its 1970s bands, who sang praises of the grid-like road system over hypnotically repetitive drum patterns? Can they be entirely disentangled?

You're aware that Edinburgh, now looming on the horizon in the form of the slumbering lion, Arthur's Seat, is the place from which Scottish Dictator Hamish McPherson planned to take over the world back in the 1930s. Had he won his wars of conquest, McPherson would have renamed the city 'Edinburgh Scotia' and rebuilt it in gargantuan proportions as the capital of the world.

You've seen scale models of the vast dome McPherson and his architect Henry Baird planned to build atop the rock of Edinburgh Castle – a dome able to house so vast a crowd, it's said, that their collective breath, as they hymned McPherson's achievements in phrases of startling banality, would form clouds up in the cupola, clouds which would periodically drench everyone present in a drizzle of saliva.

You know, too, the train of cultural ideas that led to McPherson's ascent – his admiration for the German Romantic movement, his early exposure to Scottish philosopher David Reynard Meekle, who preached that God was dead and that fierce clans of warrior-poets should descend from the Scottish mountains to grasp the reins of the world's destiny in their rough, pure hands.

McPherson was defeated, of course, and as a result the fields of East Lothian are in the hands of the communists. You can glimpse this zone from the A1 corridor, but you're not allowed to enter the alien landscape without a visa. Nevertheless, your transit somehow leaves the motorway and you find yourself – without the necessary paperwork

– in the heart of socialist-controlled Scotland, somewhere near a military base.

You and Sonic Flower Groove play football on a spookily quiet village green after paying foreign currency for bottles of Irn-Bru, the fizzy orange socialist drink. A framed portrait of the current Scottish chancellor, Ken Currie, gazes down at you from the wall behind the cash desk, thin-lipped. Not wishing to push his luck, Crusher, the tour manager, herds you back into the van after half an hour and you're soon approaching the free Western zone of Edinburgh, a city still divided by a notorious wall between its Old and New Town.

As the first boxy Modernist towers of the city of Edinburgh begin to define the horizon – all the old buildings were, of course, destroyed by intensive air raids – Guinness and a hanger-on named Halibut are playing T. Rex on a ghetto blaster. The batteries are running down, so the music wheezes and woozes across the tape heads. 'Can't you put that out of its misery?' you snap. But the boys, like schoolyard toughs, just grin broadly from the back seat. They're probably on drugs. They don't seem to care much about arriving in the capital for the first time.

For you, though, it's an incredibly exciting moment. You can't forget that German rock star David Bowie moved to the Scottish capital in 1977, after Los Angeles and cocaine had nearly ruined him, when he thought the devil lived in his swimming pool and deliriously declared in interviews that he was destined to become the next chancellor of Germany. He lived above an auto repair shop in the rough, arty district of Stockbridge, mixing freely with the Pakistani immigrants who defined the place. There he recorded a trilogy of albums – now considered the pinnacle of his experimental work – at Castle Sound Studios, within sight of Edinburgh Castle where McPherson had planned to build his world-governing dome. Bowie even called the infamous dictator 'the first rock star' and praised his gestural choreography.

In your head, thanks to Bowie, Edinburgh already has a certain sound. It's the dark, romantic din, shard-sharp, of urban alienation and glamorous despair; something metallic, alcoholic, clanging, tinny, robotic, exotic, utterly Scottish. But now that you're actually in the city, you discover this sound is also a smell – the smell of breweries on a misty night, when yellow sodium streetlights flare and a dim gloss of rain sheens the dark stone of terraces divided by the Wall.

And it is misty when – leaving Sonic Flower Groove in a Lothian Road youth hostel to fuck their groupies, snort speed, and fart freely – you catch an underground train to Granton, eager to experience the place that Bowie named an instrumental after.

It's disappointing; there's nothing there but damp walls, chimneys disappearing into low clouds, the lights of a distant sports stadium, small planes on their final approach to the nearby airfield, and the acrid smell of hops. But somehow the mythology invests even this sullen dullness with mystical significance.

After your show (at a discotheque called Clouds, somewhere in the warren of streets near the Grassmarket) the rest of the band heads back down the A1 corridor towards the ferry that will return them to Germany. But you elect to spend your concert fee on a week in Edinburgh. The city has cast its spell on you, and a pretty student called Daniella has taken you under her wing. You watch Rohmer films together and visit an exhibition about the city's chequered history called 'Edinburgh! Edinburgh!'

The following day you get a day pass to visit the communist sector and – like Michael Caine in a Cold War spy thriller – walk up Waterloo Place, avoiding the currency touts, to the shopping arcade in the St James Centre. Here, drab socialist citizens queue in the rain outside bookshops, and shoe shops display a handful of dated utilitarian styles. It's a different world, a world of proletarian crowds in malls seeking cheap electronic goods and mass-produced food. You buy a loaf marked 'Milanda' and wonder how it can even be defined as bread: white strips with the consistency of soggy cardboard peel off one by one, blocking your throat with ungulpable gobs of pulpy glue.

You sit in an enormous canteen drinking banana liquor, watching groups of black American soldiers who've come here for Rest & Recreation. They've bought enormous crates of the cheap state-produced whisky which is socialist Scotland's main export. Something about them reminds you of extras in the movies of Stan Douglas, which in turn reminds you of another purchase Scotland has on your imagination: in the 1970s, the Scottish New Wave produced some of the most interesting cinema made anywhere. Back when you were a student, your shelves heaved with glossy coffee table books filled with moody photographs of Sean Connery as a conquistador on an Amazonian raft, Ronnie Corbett as Dracula, and Alex Harvey driving a Hillman Imp across Scotland with his daughter, to a soundtrack featuring Slik, The Bay City Rollers and The Average White Band.

As the day begins to fade, unable to find the crossing point dividing socialist Waterloo Place from capitalist Princes Street, you ask a flower seller how to get to the West End. He looks startled. 'Ah, for that you will need a visa,' he says.

Tacked to the tarpaulin wall of his flower stall you see the obligatory image of thin-lipped Ken Currie, and beside it a snapshot of one of the bombastic murals the leader used to make before becoming a politician. In it, heroic fishermen bring record catches from the North Sea, heroic mothers push heroic prams, heroic farmers drive enormous tractors over the gorse-lined hills of East Lothian, and heroic chemists hold test tubes high in their laboratories.

For a moment you consider staying in this Scottish socialist utopia forever. In three years, it will be gone.

SCOTLAND 151

There is widespread condemnation of the security barrier the English have erected around Scotland, but – despite the fact that it is in clear breach of international law, violates human rights, and causes unnecessary suffering to the Scottish people – very little is done about it. Motions in condemnation of the situation are presented constantly at the UN, only to be vetoed by England and its allies.

The English assert that the barrier, which follows the contours of Hadrian's Wall, is necessary to prevent the Scots from carrying out terrorist atrocities on English soil. Meanwhile, their policy of secretly assassinating leading Scottish intellectuals in exile continues.

The Scottish poet Walter Auzie, living in exile in Rome at the time of his death, was the first casualty of this covert programme carried out by the English secret service, or ESOP. Auzie was gunned down in the hallway of his apartment on October 16th, 1972. It was the first in a series of reprisals for the killing of eleven members of the English team at the Munich Olympic Games a month before.

Why ESOP chose a cultural figure – a poet – is not clear. It may very well have been a case of mistaken identity.

Like many Scots in exile (and almost all poets), Auzie lived a modest life. He would rise at around seven, write until eleven or so, drink coffee in a nearby café, take a simple lunch alone or with friends, and visit the library to lose himself in the works of Gaelic and Scots dialect poets. He made a new Italian translation of Ossian's *Fingal* while in Rome.

Auzie also helped edit *Rivoluzione Scozzese*, an Italian language magazine which supported the Scottish uprising. The offices of *Rivoluzione Scozzese* —where Auzie served as literary editor – were on the Via Giulia, and it was here the poet spent his afternoons, in a small room overlooking the Tiber, shaded by Scots Pines.

His poetry earned him no money, so Auzie was forced to work as an extra at nearby Cinecitta – he played, for instance, one of the pirate crew aboard Lichas' ship in Fellini's 1969 film *Satyricon*. The evening ESOP agents pumped twelve bullets into him – one for each of the English athletes killed in Munich, some say, and one for himself – Auzie had been making phone calls in the Trieste Bar below his seventh floor apartment, where the electricity and phone line had been cut off. With a meanness which was typically Scottish, Auzie simply hadn't paid his bills.

Auzie's tragic end was revisited at the 2007 Venice Biennale, in a room of the Italian pavilion where an artist called Amelie Pantir assembled 'material for a film' about Auzie's life: photographs of him in Rome, clips of his appearances as an extra, copies of *Rivoluzione Scozzese* encased in vitrines, a collection of his private letters, and a panel featuring covers of books in his library: paperbacks by Jean Genet, Schopenhauer, Engels, Eliot, Kierkegaard and Pound.

A volume of Ossian's *Fingal*, carried in Auzie's breast pocket on the evening of his assassination, still has embedded within its spine a single bullet from the .22 pistols fired by the English agents.

SCOTLAND 38

The Scotland which is China's Airstrip One, and hosts her intercontinental ballistic missiles.

SCOTLAND 89

The Scotland in which every schoolchild can recite, by heart, the table talk of R.D. Laing.

SCOTLAND 156

The Scotland in which bluebirds are flying... in the cellar... even blackbirds are extinct... somewhere... high in the sky.

SCOTLAND 107

Schools, offices, mortgages and cars don't really exist for the Scots; somehow they've diverted the things that preoccupy the rest of us and pared their lives down to bare essentials. They subsist without visible means of support, seeming to live on air, water and febrile nerves.

It takes a while to adjust to the nervous energy of the Scots. Their society is constantly bombarded with information – not from above, but rather from below, from the grassroots. Trends come and go in the twinkling of an eye, and everyone has a hand in it. Behind the façades of musty, gritty bohemian terraces, Scottish life is a scintillating string of inventions garlanded with witty *bons mots*.

A middle-aged lady in a shabby café might be wearing limited edition Lucha Libre retro basketball shoes and a Mexican wrestling mask while working on a script for a film she'll shoot with a cheap digicam. A kid nearby is building a paper helicopter that really flies. Two bearded twins are talking about the links between cacti and calculus. Everyone seems super-bright, slightly neurotic, and joyfully intense.

Barter is widely practised, and most people live without bank accounts or, for that matter, incomes. They rarely leave the locality, and yet the whole world seems to come to them through the air, intellectually.

When acquaintances meet on Edinburgh's George Street there's immediately a flurry of enquiries about 'projects'.

'How's your passive action project? Great to hear! Oh, my liquorice graveyard project is going well, over a dozen stones now, we have the launch on Friday, it'd be great to see you there! Bring Lachlan! And Rose! You're still together? Oh, with both of them? Wonderful!'

None of these projects are commercial in any way. The Scots are post-money. They live for experience, for collaboration, for networking, for the intense sociability of the art opening, for the pleasures of the moment. They do everything without payment, just for the sake of doing it. Most grow their own food on allotments, some live in geodesic greenhouses. No gallery reception is complete without the ritual exchange of cabbage and cauliflower.

Scots seem always to be chewing gum; in fact it's a natural drug similar to khat, and it keeps them hyper-alert and sharp. They call it 'chaumy' and grow it on their allotments to trade on the black market or to pass around their friends.

Many Scots smoke chaumy pipes in the dive bars called Chaumy Lairs. You can go to an Edinburgh Chaumy Lair at any hour of the night or day and a skeletal Scot with red, hollow, burning eyes will engage you immediately in debate about life, art and politics, for as long as you like. The storytellers, machars, will make you roar with laughter with one of the shaggy dog stories they call 'bloont plooms'.

A Scottish party is only getting going at 6 or 7am, and won't wind down until the next day, so take a packed lunch — and breakfast just in case.

You might think that this bohemian intensity would slow when couples have children, but not a bit of it: people just take their kids wherever they go, and if the parents stay up three days in a row, the kids do too.

Scots all seem of indeterminate age, but essentially they stay young forever and then, unexpectedly, they die. When this happens, nobody makes a fuss. The person's absence at the most fashionable parties is duly noted, and a curt explanation provided: 'Oh, Stuart died. It happens to the best of us, I hear.'

My time in Edinburgh passed in a whirlwind of parties under vast paper lanterns. I remember church cellars twinkling with artificial blossoms, beaches dotted with improvising dancers, sheep farmers piping their flocks across urban mountains, reciting epic poetry. Brilliant chatter rings in my ears, turns of phrase I will never forget, glimpses of profoundest wisdom lightly told, sexual encounters followed by food which tasted better than anything I've ever eaten.

Truly, the precious filament of existence burns more brightly in that happy land. I am convinced that every Scot has grasped the most salient and mysterious fact of being, its glowing ruby kernel: the knowledge that life rewards those who love – but really love – to live.

SCOTLAND 120

The Scotland which becomes the world's first successful post-industrial matriarchy.

SCOTLAND 41

The Scotland in which a thousand flowers bloom, and a thousand schools of thought contend.

SCOTLAND 62

To whom it may concern:

I am Paul Younger, the artist.

Scotland has asked me to provide her with a testimonial letter detailing our activities, together with my recommendation that she be permitted to remain in Great Britain for a further period of one year.

Scotland provided me with invaluable assistance during the preparation and performance of my action 'Five in One' at the Zurich Triennial last year. She not only lent essential logistical support (assisting the public, making cups of tea, helping me erect the teepee, feeding the lemur and stringing together one hundred antique telephones into an ersatz exchange), but she also took part in the brainstorming sessions that allowed me to crystallise the actions, events, context, content and duration of the performance.

We live in a time of post-post-colonial globalization, the cultural era Nicolas Bourriaud has called the 'Altermodern'. It is a point-to-point, multipolar world set free from the old unipolar globalization of the New World Order. In this world, where communication exists on a many-to-many, rhizomic palimpsest, old Modernisms are effaced and new ones inscribed – less essentialist, less Western-oriented.

Working with Scotland, often late into the night, I arrived at the visual metaphor of the exchange as the perfect form for the installation. Alexander Graham Bell's invention of the telephone – the template for all supervening technologically mediated communication grids – was our paradigmatic metonym. The lemur sat on top.

Much of the coverage of the Zurich Triennial singled out The Exchange as worthy of mention, and the piece boosted not only my own career, but also the perception of Zurich as a town of cultural relevance. I would argue that an ancillary effect of the exhibition's success (32,000 entries over its three week span) was the heightened awareness of Great Britain as a valuable 'interrogator' on the global stage, a maker of tentative – yet firm! – interventions.

It would be a great injustice if, after all this, personable, charming, capable and intelligent Scotland were to be expelled from the United Kingdom. She has, I believe, as much to offer your project as she offered mine.

Yours sincerely,
Paul Younger,
Artist

SCOTLAND 42

The Scotland in which the flowers wilt, and the schools agree.

SCOTLAND 34

Craiglinton the Elder was born in Linlithgow. It was his family's intention to set him to smithery like his father, well-known in that town for his metal skills. But Craiglinton so devoted himself to the art of the chisel, and the results were so widely remarked and admired, that it was decided he should follow instead the calling, divinely ordained, of sculpture.

Craiglinton first marked himself out as a prodigious child when he created, in the space of just three weeks, a team of farm animals so realistic that passers-by could not bring themselves to believe the beasts did not live and breathe. The animals were hewn out of white sandstone, then painted in manifold colours by a technique unknown to any other artists at that time. In order to keep his methods secret the sculptor laboured long into the night, bringing forth forms from soft rock, standing barefoot in his father's smithy in the freezing winter weather, surrounded by the cooing turtle doves which were his constant companions.

When the work was unveiled, the town guild offered Craiglinton his own studio and two assistants, and the Duke of Portobello gave him a fixed allowance of fifteen Scottish ducats a month, a small fortune at that time. In gratitude, Craiglinton carved the magnificent equestrian statue of the Duke that now dominates Musselburgh's jewellery district. He also made a reclining shepherd for the Temple of Pan at Cramond and a series of Madonna and Child pieces, of exquisite grace and modesty, for the pious Lady Helena Fairfax of Scone.

Craiglinton's fame soon exceeded the boundaries of Scotland, and he was invited by the courts of many foreign potentates to decorate their palaces and chapels with his magnificent figures, unparalleled in subtlety and grace. It was on one of these voyages overseas, however, that Craiglinton caught a fever and was claimed by that dark exciseman who carries off the best of us, and our gifts too.

At the time of his death, Craiglinton was generously assisted by his eldest son Pierrot Craiglinton, whose abilities almost matched, already, the exquisite peaks attained by his father. Known as Craiglinton the Younger,

Pierrot completed all his father's outstanding commissions. Then, over the next twenty years, by many feats and constant work, he established himself as Scotland's foremost carver, extending his father's forms into precious metals such as bronze, silver and gold.

It was Pierrot, of course, who created the famous frieze of Saint Agnes Kilda slaying the yellow stag, and made the marvellous sculpture of the Battle of Glenlurgo, which included six hundred separate pieces, each one at half the scale of life. At sunset the sight is magnificent, for the shiny metal glisters in Phoebus' sinking rays, so that one may imagine the pine forest alive with celestial soldiers.

It is to the family name of Craiglinton that we must attribute the genius sufficient to the making of these marvels, which, to this day, have not been matched in Scotland.

When Pierrot himself was at last an old man with a full beard, buskins and snow sandals, it became clear to all that he would not survive another winter. And so Laird John of Menzies decreed that the artist should be commemorated in a giant statue bestriding the Water of Leith near Balerno. Envoys were sent up and down Scotland to find the sculptor who could achieve such a travail, but not one was suitable for such a difficult and important task.

Finally Pierrot himself was prevailed upon to execute the commission, despite a severe case of arthritis. Throughout September, October and November, Pierrot could be seen lying flat on his back on a wooden scaffolding high above the rapids of the Water of Leith, hacking at a gigantic piece of stone which had been transported by elephant teams from the quarries of Norway. As he worked, Pierrot was surrounded by his assistants and his beloved turtle doves.

Alas, he was only able to complete the netherparts of his own anatomy; his legs and the underside of his groin. One morning in early December Pierrot was found frozen, his hammer raised to the hanging stone testicle sac, his eyes glassy and dull as two beads.

Rigor mortis and the icy weather had finally transformed Pierrot himself into a sculpture.

In this melancholy way, it is said, he completed the commission laid upon him by the Laird John of Menzies, though not as either man would have wished. Some say it was the gigantic self-portrait which killed him, and a few of those blame the Laird. But all agree that Pierrot died as he was surely destined to, at work on marvels.

We shall not see his like again. But his likeness, left deliberately half-completed in tribute to him, straddles the rapids at Balerno to this day. There is not one Scottish sculptor of recent times who has not gone there and knelt to touch the stone, hoping to be filled, by osmosis, with Pierrot's gifts, and those of his dear father, Craiglinton the Elder.

SCOTLAND 97

The Scotland in which the monarch is Aslan and the glen is Narnia.

SCOTLAND 153

The Scotland in which the witch is Tilda.

SCOTLAND 52

The Scotland turned – because of its low population levels – into a vast particle accelerator bowling alley, with the skittles at Thurso.

SCOTLAND 39

In this Scotland, the now erases the now. People are so attuned to the differences between this moment and every other – differences constantly monitored via a stream of little updates running through their occipital implants – that their 'now' has become a vigil without object, a watch without event. Primed at each moment for movements of the moment itself, the Scots find themselves unable to see, to feel, and to act.

Ask them tomorrow what happened yesterday and they will hush you with an impatient gesture: some information is coming in about possible changes to the moment, and you are disturbing it! When the update is done – it was nothing important, finally – they will tell you that yesterday they were doing what they did today: waiting for a dispatch which would change the shape of things definitively, a dispatch shaped like the one that just came in, but more significant. In fact, the importance of this awaited update cannot be emphasised enough!

And so the Scots pass their days in a permanent state of readiness for an earth-shattering event which never occurs. This readiness is all that concerns them. For some it is a spiritual matter, like preparation for death or the return of a long-promised messiah.

'Have you received the message?' the pious ask each other. 'Not yet,' comes the reply, 'but I have a feeling it could come today, even in the next moment.' And they mist over, these Scots, as they focus on the status chips they've had voluntarily implanted in their brains (at considerable expense to themselves, and not a little pain). In the absence of content, they pay close attention to form; the rhythm the updates make, the colours they associate with each blip, the density of the information in each spasm.

Much has been lost in this recalibration to an empty moment. Sustained attention, love, serious works of art, a sense of humour, a sense of perspective, the joys of the body, the satisfactions of physical labour – everything has been swept away by an occipital surf which brings nothing, wave on wave, to the shore of consciousness.

There is some justice in the stereotype of the Scots as a grey people, a grave people, and a grim one. For, poised forever on the brink of a discovery which never comes, they are nowhere, and live without joy or gratification. They are ascetics without the consolation of knowledge, priests without a god, fanatics without a hobby, fetishists without an obsession. They stand forever on the edge of a grey ocean, but will never feel its icy water on their skin. They haven't even noticed the gulls. But don't try to tell them the error of their ways; halfway through, the Scots will hush you with an urgent, impatient gesture – some information is coming in! And this time it really could be important.

SCOTLAND 123

The Buddhist Scotland. Nam Myōhō Renge Kyō!

SCOTLAND 83

I was queuing for hours at the library. We all were, waiting to get to the cash machines. You had to queue several times. The first time you just got the card, then the second time you got an authorisation code, then the third time you could actually get the cash. In the queue I read a notebook I'd picked up. It contained conversations written in a club so loud the human voice couldn't be heard. One of the participants was a Japanese girl, a rich scion of a banking family. I decided that later I would get in touch with her using the email address she had written down.

People were drifting away from the library, towards the halls of residence. I felt a bit odd about that, with all the money in my pocket. In a corridor I joked with the boss while trying to pull a protector over my head. I perforated the neck brace along the dotted line, but couldn't make the two halves fit. Eventually I left the 'cloakroom' with a skateboard instead of the cardboard canopy I was supposed to be wearing.

Skateboarding down Princes Street, I was surprised to see police cars. So I decided to take The Mound and skate down home through the Old Town. A patrol car passed me as I climbed the towpath. It was broadcasting a message about casuals from Portobello, warning people to take care. When I reached the top of The Mound, where the ground slopes steeply away to the south, I discovered that the cobbled road was being dug up. It would be impossible to skate down.

I looked into a theatre museum in a Milanese garden halfway down the hill, carrying my skateboard and taking pictures rapidly of all the exhibits. One of the urbane visitors thought I was a secret policeman. When I got back outside, I was slightly lost; I could see the craggy black cliff of the castle arching round and back down to the New Town, but that wasn't the right road to take.

So instead I went up to the very top, that scary place where there's a rail junction, an underground motorway, and the road to the pier. I was standing on the narrow pavement beside the motorway bridge when I saw Pete and Marie, two friends. We laughed about how scary that place was, when the junction swung around and there was no room anywhere, and the train passed by. I told Pete and Marie I was taking the ferry down the Thames Estuary.

The pier opened up. A man ahead of me was swallowed by a patch of sandy whiteness where the road and the pier met. I resolved not to step on that.

The people waiting to board the ferry were waterlogged. At one point I started getting swept away from them, into the freezing river. 'Help! Help!' I shouted, but a couple of breast strokes set me on course for the entrance to the boat, and soon I could board.

Inside, floor-to-ceiling windows filled the stark vessel with an Arctic light. We were all to sleep on a raised platform packed with 'swaddling', multicoloured cables of wool which looked like huge fabric candies. These would ensure that our body temperatures remained high enough during the voyage.

There was a blizzard outside, and visibility seemed dangerously low. As the Thames became more crowded, I could see other vessels very close to ours. Eventually we reached the centre of the city, where huge imperial buildings shaped like the Atari logo rose in red brick, and somehow looked upside-down. There were also bronze corporate sculptures everywhere.

The city felt very rich, Roman-Japanese. Shizu and I were ushered into a taxi by her parents, who were unimaginably wealthy business people. We dismounted in a crowded, prosperous area near some wrought iron theatre buildings. I almost left the notebook in the back of the taxi. The driver spoke some formal phrases in English before driving off.

We were ushered through the home belonging to Shizu's parents – where we'd be staying from now on – into the corporate garden behind. There were corporate rose-beds and abstract bronze sculptures. I could see St Paul's cathedral and other London landmarks, but this was Tokyo. Everything was enormous, made of brick, and upside down. I liked it here. Shizu and I would inherit this empire when her parents died.

SCOTLAND 53

The Scotland in which people walk naked down George Street and around the corner into Charlotte Square.

SCOTLAND 14

The Scotland in which Irn-Bru really is brewed 'from girders'.

SCOTLAND 166

The Scotland ruled – from a massive lighthouse in Pollockshaws – by an ancient, sleekit, decrepit Rudolf Hess parachuted into Glasgow from a Messerschmitt.

SCOTLAND 143

The new Sonic Flower Groove album *MVCCVM* breaks little new ground – and why should it?

Like all their other releases – and most major world religions – it preaches the values of Modesty, Virtue, Compassion, Consideration, Vulnerability and Moderation (which is the meaning of the title's palindromic acronym, by the way).

The band's main influences continue to be Donovan and The Incredible String Band, their sound a delicate cat's cradle of acoustic instruments imported from their travels in Morocco and Afghanistan.

The results are gently aromatic; the kind of music you

want to listen to in the lotus position, halfway up some metaphorical mountain on a path to spiritual awakening. Personally, I listened to MVCCVM while crushing garlic cloves and pulsed pine nuts into a bowl of basil pesto, as six dear friends from diverse ethnic backgrounds conversed around a nearby dinner table.

On opening track 'Boddisatva' Billy Gethsemane chants the song's title like a mantra, his hair swishing audibly around the microphone. This ode to a dawning awareness of his own 'Buddha nature' becomes a hypnotic drone worthy of Enya.

The second song is called 'The Middle Kingdom', and preaches the value of moderation in all things. 'Avoid excess, even as you avoid that excess we call avoidance,' Gethsemane intones, wisely, while Innes bows a sitar and Mani squeezes a shruti box with tactful restraint.

The ten-minute epic 'Trance and Transcendence' follows, a tapestry of glissandos, an impassioned plea for compassion even – especially – for those who think and feel differently than we do. You may have heard it on television during the recent Public Meditation on Tibet.

And so, like a slow, mighty river meandering down from mountains to the sea, the album thunders to its poignant, touching end, with the warm, glowing shingle sounds of 'Everlasting Tassle' tickling the cockles of our ears like a gently receding tide.

Everything here is measured, poised and tasteful. It's no less than we've come to expect from Sonic Flower Groove.

Just one thing disturbs me, however. This is a Scottish

group, and recent reports have revealed the extent to which female genital mutilation is still practised in Scotland.

Yet nowhere on this admittedly beautiful album do Billy and the boys stop to address this moral outrage. Their silence leaves a bad taste in my mouth. Although I personally do not blame the band for clitorectomy, and although I am sure they neither practise nor advocate genital cutting, their silence on the subject seems provocative.

It is not a virtue to tolerate the intolerable. And it is not right to pass in silence over the silence with which Scotland continues this abhorrent tradition. By presenting such a mild, wise and gentle face to the world, are Sonic Flower Groove not distorting the public impression of Scotland? Are they not whitewashing? Are they not, finally, complicit?

In view of this worrisome omission – this deafening silence – I have docked one star from the rating I am awarding this fine album. I sincerely hope Sonic Flower Groove will clarify their position with regard to genital cutting on their next record.

SCOTLAND 99

The Scotland in which ginger-haired people are discovered to be a distinct species: *Jocko Homo*.

SCOTLAND 114

The Scotland in which the national dress is the polka-dot poncho, of course.

SCOTLAND 103

'A computer makes a Scotland seem almost unnecessary,' says the famous performance artist, now an architect. 'If you can have all the information in front of you on a computer, do you need the actual Scotland? The notions of a Scotland now don't seem as separate from notions of 'England' and notions of 'Europe' as they used to. 'Scotland' is seen to be spreading… maybe a Scotland starts to be more portable. If you can carry all the information from a Scotland, does that mean you carry the Scotland with you rather than going into a Scotland? Does each person now have the possibility of carrying a portable Scotland rather than installing himself or herself in an actual Scotland?'

SCOTLAND 88

Once upon a time it seemed easier to be both a foreigner and a good object for the Scots. In the 1990s young Scots were more open to foreign travel, to collaborations with foreigners on equal terms. Scots you might meet abroad are still these people – widely travelled and broad-minded, cosmopolitan, outward-looking.

But something has changed within Scotland itself. Since arriving at Findhorn I've been keenly aware of a surprising new mood here, an intensely inward-looking mood akin to narcissism. Scotland, increasingly, performs itself to itself as 'the other', an exotic tourist destination primped for internal consumption.

Television here in the Highlands is an endless advertorial presentation of winter resorts where Scottish families go to marvel at intensely, even stereotypically, Scottish wonders; to hunt grouse and stag, to curl, to fish for salmon, to play golf, to hike in the mountains, and to retreat to spiritual resorts to study under a guru. If the air route between Edinburgh and Inverness has become the most heavily used flightpath in the world, it's partly because of 'spiritual traffic'.

I had dinner on Friday night with some twenty-year-old Scottish kids – students of the Future University – and asked them some questions. None of them had been outside Scotland, and none seemed very keen to travel. They planned to spend their whole lives here in the Highlands.

Although I'm sad that the current Scottish mood of intense self-love seems not to embrace me in quite the same way as 1990s global postmodern Scottish culture did, I'm generally positive about the trend toward national narcissism. I believe Scotland really does have a culture worth protecting, celebrating, and being proud of. It's a sensual culture, a refined and beautiful culture. It contains radically different, particular and valuable ways of thinking, feeling, tasting, seeing, embracing, bathing, being. I want Scottish people, rather than tourists, to be the curators of this culture, and I believe that foreigners will benefit from there being a 'Scottish way of being' even if they seem excluded from it (by the huge cost of holidays here, the difficulties in negotiating Scotland's rather foreigner-unfriendly infrastructure, and the strong blood ties of clans to each other).

Watching Highlands television last night, I saw Scottishness being performed for a domestic audience in the form of travelogues and internal tourism puffs. The evening's viewing was a parade of beautiful, archetypical Scottish experiences being marvelled at by Scottish people as if they were foreigners in their own country. Narcissism, after all, implies both self-love and a certain self-alienation. Can that lovely face looking up from the pool really be me?

Love, even self-love, often starts off as a lie. But it's a virtuous and transformative lie; a lie that might just become the truth. If you believe contentment is something good, something a nation should aspire to, you have to accept that self-contentment might be a perfectly reasonable way to achieve it.

And – here's the point – I have an inkling that this self-alienation is the point at which foreigners can insert themselves into Scotland. Because, if the Scots need Scotland performed for them as an exotic spectacle, they're already foreigners in their own land. The Scots are almost Scottish. And so am I.

SCOTLAND 27

The Scotland in which Gaelic is the only official language. All signs are in Gaelic, all television broadcasts, all newspapers. Everywhere you go in this Scotland, people pretend not to understand if you address them in English.

SCOTLAND 102

The Scotland which, thanks to oil revenues, becomes much richer than England and erects an electric fence between the two countries to halt opportunistic economic migration.

SCOTLAND 140

The Scotland which sees a civil war between the roundheads and the flatheads, with the redheads acting as double agents.

SCOTLAND 127

The adjective 'Scotwellian' is a somewhat charged word, combining two authors and one country: George Orwell, Edith Sitwell, Scotland.

It has effectively come to delineate the Scotland we know today, a Scotland which has been turned into a huge, crumbling aristocratic estate policed by people dressed in the costumes of ancient Greek gods.

It is a Scotland in which – at any moment – you are probably being watched by Pan, the god of panic and pandemonium, and in which the yellow sphere poised above like an omniscient telescreen is 'Phoebus, the enormous and gold-rayed rustling sun'.

In this classical-feudal Scotland, omnisurveillance is the task of Greek deities who wander beneath urns and through gilded trellises like so many extras from a painting by Poussin. But since the autocratic aristocrats who run the land are waspishly eccentric and don't care to read the reports that the pseudo-deities write, all that results is poetry. It's as if the Thought Police were shaggy-legged satyrs chasing each other up and down the spiral staircases of corbelled turrets jutting over the squinch arches of monumental doorways.

In Scotwellian Scotland, most of us live in feudal cottages arranged around the outer walls of the great estates. We supply our deluded overlords with service, tithes, and food. Our masters once hunted stag in the forest, and built fortifications to resist the Danes. But this generation has fallen into effete, decadent desuetude, preferring to write sonnets which they perform, prancing amongst shrubbage of *Rhododendron ponticum* down by the pseudo-Grecian folly at the end of the larch avenue, on the longest night of summer.

We, the peasantry, are surveyed not through cameras but by an invited audience of dabblers and dilettantes who enjoy amateur dramatics. With a purple diplax draped across a white chiton, we are forced to hold a ridiculous position for hours, a heavy lyre in each hand, representing The Rescue of Pyrrhus or The Noble Deed of Scipio or The Triumph of Neptune and Amphitrite.

When we return to our thatched hovels and tear off flimsy garments better suited to Patras than Partick, we complain bitterly about our Scotwellian treatment. Didn't the Greeks – aside from the endless gods who flounce about Scotland's endless estates during the endless days of an endless midsummer – didn't the Greeks also invent a thing called democracy?

But anyone who knows the Sitwells will know that they associate democracy with *la trahison des clercs*, and with the inexpressible vulgarity of a world – they shudder to think of it – in which every Scot would drive a car, and all of Scotland would be carpet warehouses and DIY garden centres.

(There is more to write, but it is time to gather near the beehives for the Two Minutes' Hate against Noel Coward.)

SCOTLAND 69

The Scotland in which geese permanently block the sky, and seethe over the ground as far as the eye can see.

SCOTLAND 75

The Scotland in which all food is soup.

SCOTLAND 74

The Scotland in which nobody has any teeth.

SCOTLAND 157

The visitor to Scotland is likely to be shocked by the incredible scenes of poverty that will greet him at every turn. From the moment the Scots ascertain that he is from another land, the tourist will be dogged by beggars.

In order to keep these questers at bay, it is wise to employ a 'gillie' who can communicate with the greedy, famished brutes who follow, haunting the visitor with plaintive cries. The gillie will beat them, constantly and without mercy, with a stout stick. The problem is that not all gillies are honest; in many cases the 'protector' turns out to be a greater menace than the rabble of thieves he claims to protect against. The medicine, so to speak, is worse than the disease.

You may be tempted to ride in a 'scrutter', a sort of Scottish rickshaw held at shoulder height. But be aware that scrutter-runners have been known to divert suddenly into a close and deprive their passenger of his choicest valuables.

If such a thing happens to you, above all do not go to the police; as a rule of thumb, the higher you go in Scotland, the more corrupt and venial the people become. If you lose one hundred dubloons to a street ruffian, you will certainly lose a thousand in the attempt to report it, and ten thousand if you take the matter to court. Persist to the Court of Appeal and you will be lucky to escape with your life; if there is talk of spies and treachery abroad in the land at that time, be sure that you will be blamed, and it will not be long before hanging and lynching are discussed. Nothing less will placate the mob.

Nevertheless, despite the almost complete breakdown in trust, I will say – and this may surprise you – that the Scots are some of the most hospitable and generous people that I have ever had the good fortune to meet. If you need accommodation while walking in the popular quarters of a Scottish town, you will certainly be offered full bed and board by a simple family, who will empty the most crowded room just to give you the quiet night's sleep they believe you deserve. They will even, without being bidden, send their prettiest daughter to sweeten your stay. And should you leave her with child, they will consider the babe a generous gift.

It is for this reason that many foreigners have left their hearts in Scotland; once they learn the ways of the Scots, they never wish to leave. In fact some have stayed, renting – for next to nothing – large, handsome houses in picturesque squares thronging with rude vitality.

You will recognize these expatriates by their broad-brimmed hats, capes and canes, by the way they walk past arrogantly, scrupulously avoiding your gaze, and by their icy coldness when addressed. For Scotland is a secret they do not wish to share, above all with their own kind.

These naturalised foreigners are one of the greatest dangers you will face during your stay, for they will think nothing of frightening a fellow foreigner away – if tales told in a dark tavern over a brass pot of ale will not suffice, why, they will wait outside at closing time with a cutlass and a couple of hooligans.

What these desperate exiles fear most is having their paradise broken into by one of their own kind, or – heaven forbid! – a multitude of their own kind. Each wishes to be unique, 'the only foreigner in Scotland', and to receive – alone! – the generous attentions of the Scots, their tender curiosity, even their violence and rapacity. For it is at heart a kind of masochism to hate your own kind, and to value only the love given you by the strangers who surround you.

It is said that some of these jealous foreigners cannot even stand the sight of a mirror. If you are pursued by one, be sure to find a full-length mirror which can be swung between yourself and your pursuer; a wardrobe or bathroom door will do, or the mirrored screens of a fancy tavern. The foreigner will stop, raise his hands in horror against his own reflection, and fall hissing to the cobbles, foaming at the mouth.

For the exile's own image will shatter the perceived perfection of his adopted land, a perfection that depends, above all, on his own absence from it.

SCOTLAND 21

An introductory walk in the city by myself. The vigour, the bodies, the deadly playfulness of the traffic; these things haven't yet worked any erotic, problematical magic on me. I expect it isn't real enough yet.

To me, Edinburgh is a memory confirming itself. To it, I'm a shade – possibly monied. The skeletal beggar women with clutching monkey children approach. I give a sympathetic, ambiguous flick of the wrist. My shirt doesn't conceal my ribcage. Jowly-faced sentries toy with their black and blue metal guns. At a certain point, as you pass, the barrel stares into your midriff.

A collision at the top of Leith Walk. The drivers clench and point and vent almost humourously. No damage has been done, but their cars are at apocalyptic angles across the street and they play the crash for all it's worth.

Near St. Andrew Square a splay-legged beauty on a moped gives me a slight internal lurch. We do not warrant one another's serious attention, but I'm piqued.

I am a botched organism with a comic shield of pride; a shield I pick at like a scab, and delight to fatigue.

Minto's new novel is about an old communist who understands and likes the young party members determined to kill him. He puts himself under a tram to keep their hands free of blood. I find this sort of thing sentimental and puritanical, but it's glamorous.

A fork lightning storm in the early hours. I fling open windows and shutters to watch as the rain comes. A couple of strong flashes set off car alarms which sound until morning. Three of these electronic screamers together sound like the run-off groove on *Taking Tiger Mountain*.

A few hours after our train crossed the bridge between Berwick-upon-Tweed and Scotland on Tuesday, a bomb exploded. Right-wing indiscriminate killing. Luckily it misfired.

Wrote a page of *Pang's Compass* on Minto's electric typewriter. Bellowesque. Bobby criticises its density. But it doesn't bore me.

Walk. Japanese tourists at the Castle Esplanade. St. Giles in light (marbled light, eerie light) against a lazily forking thundercloud. What I value most here are the nimble, saturnine and above all mortal faces of the Scots. Sheltering from the downpour in a church, I study crude shop-window Catholic dummies with incised stigmata. Stanley Cursiter's gashed canvases must derive from these waxy Christs' chests.

I'm comforted by the universally asthenic representation of the Saviour. It makes me feel better about my nipple advertisement of a shirt.

On the way home after we've seen his mother off, Bobby says: 'I can very well imagine you living here.'

Edinburgh in August is hot and vacant, incredibly so. The shops say 'closed for the holidays'. It's like a seaside town in winter. So botched wretches like me lie cupping our novels (which begin to annoy us with their crammed lives of event, thought and love), sweating into our trousers. Or visit the zoo, where silver-haired, spotty-pated chimpanzees slump in green barred rooms, picking at husks. '*Sehr schlecht*,' says a German woman.

Visitors to zoos are often more bored than the inmates. They stand watching apes in the concrete pit. The apes romp and stare back. A Japanese couple smiles with parental indulgence. Two old apes square like sumo wrestlers. A plump sadist lights a cigarette and flicks the match, still lit, down at *Macacca Mulatta*. Each pit is a littered version of *Endgame*, with occasional slapstick. I walk away relieved, walk myself stupid, walk till the basic appetites rear up like familiar, comforting headlands: rest, food, sex.

I visit a clogged market, cross the North Bridge and see the gasworks, comfortably ugly. The reality principle. Calton Hill is a pleasant place from which to watch Bellow's Charlie Citrine fly the Atlantic, but traces of a psychic shadow – the world's and my own – worry me. In a torn page from a ridiculous S&M mag, two naked women in leather hems grasp a blindfolded figure who dangles a droll white penis, long and uninterested. There are hypodermic syringes outside the Protestant cemetery. I dodge the ambiguous approaches of men in the park.

The Holyrood gun-toters, chatting up some baggy-shorted birds, call out: 'Is it true? Is it true?' as I pass. 'I don't speak English,' I reply, in English.

SCOTLAND 146

1. Because the sea has a top and does not fly beyond, there can be no boats.
2. Nothing stops the passenger nipping parts off a loaf and objectively watching the women.
3. The sky and other shipping are also restful to the eye.
4. What one coastline has forgotten, the other begins to remember.
5. Although this afternoon the young are wild, one by one they will succumb to the kitchen.
6. They will speak the jargon of the domestic back from her holiday.
7. By means of selling his information, Poseidon has become richer than ever.

SCOTLAND 116

1. Because the sea lies on top and underneath beyond, there can be no boats.
2. Nothing stops the passengers getting puffs of a loaf and objects of a rubber.
3. The sky grows an arch-shape then curled to the trees.
4. What we see is a forgotten.

MOMUS

SCOTLAND 167

Listen, I'm no conspiracy theorist – let's get that clear. I'm simply a concerned citizen who has noticed certain unmistakeable signs and patterns. Some things crop up just a little too much to be mere coincidence, right?

For example?

Well, for example, Scotland.

We talk about the society of the spectacle, the military industrial complex. What does this society – this complex – thrive on, technologically? That's right: telecommunications, television.

And who invented television, who invented the telephone? Scots did.

But that's just one piece of the jigsaw. We live in the age of fast food, of skyscrapers, of rock music – a supposedly democratic era in which these maverick values are actually imposed on us from above. But look a little closer and you'll find that all these cultural toxins have their origin in Scotland.

What are 'french fries', the staple ingredient on most fast food menus, but Scottish 'tatties' prepared in the Scots' favourite style, deep frying? And skyscrapers – everyone who visits Edinburgh is told that the high-rise tenement buildings along the Royal Mile were the world's first skyscrapers. As for rock music, sure, it might seem to be based on the blues and evangelical African-American music. But who converted the African natives to Christianity in the first place? The Scots, of course.

Scratch the hegemonic global monoculture and you'll find Scots. But it goes further than that. Much further.

Who are the meanest people in the world? Everyone knows the answer to that one. It's the Scots, and the Jews. Put them together and what do you get? You get America, my friend. The shining eye on the top of the levitating pyramid.

The Calvinist Protestantism of the Scots is at the heart of the modern capitalist system. Just read Max Weber's *The Protestant Ethic and the Spirit of Capitalism* if you doubt that. Worldly asceticism, business success as a sign of your membership in God's elect – it's all there.

James Hogg wrote a fantastic novel, *Memoirs and Confessions of a Justified Sinner*, which describes how a man is befriended by a mysterious companion, Gil-Martin, who tells him he's saved and can, as a result, kill anyone he likes with impunity. In microcosm, Hogg's novel describes the world we live in today, dominated by the alliance between the Jews and the Scots. I call that world 'Albrael'.

The Albraelis aren't just united by their meanness and their spooky intelligence, they're united by the conviction that they are God's chosen people, justified and righteous from ancient of days. So incapable are they of considering themselves sinners that they commit every sin known to man: slaughtering everyone who stands in their way, and many who don't.

Their ultimate intention? To build Jerusalem in Scotland. To achieve it, they are quite prepared to see the whole world perish in sheets of cleansing flame. For they believe that Albrael will only emerge after the final conflagration, like a phoenix rising from the global ashes.

What can we do to stop them – the Albraelis? My friend, this is the truly terrible part. There is nothing we can do. For this has all been preordained from time immemorial. All the signs and portents suggest that it will come to pass in December of 2021, when a nuclear holocaust and financial turmoil will bring the end of the current historical era. Only Scotland will survive.

Knowing this, the state of Israel will secretly begin moving its governmental machinery and its most important citizens to Edinburgh in late 2020. There will be a rapid 'Israelification' of Alba throughout that year, which will see a phantom government appear alongside the Scottish one. After the cataclysm, a new Knesset will quickly grasp the reins of power.

Hogmanay will become Rosh Hashanah, and a special mitzvah will be performed on the ramparts of Edinburgh castle as one thousand kilted rabbis blow the shofar, the ornamental ram's horn. Vegetable tithes will be calculated in turnips-per-head, and annual tree-planting duties assigned to each Albraeli. During the afternoon the Tashlikh will be recited, to the accompaniment of bagpipes. As the sound of a single trumpet note dies away, the one o'clock gun will be fired a thousand times.

SCOTLAND 118

The Scotland which African missionaries have converted to shamanic animism.

SCOTLAND 50

The Scotland in which you can see ghosts at noon, clear as day.

SCOTLAND 25

The Scotland in which new administrative regions are designated to replace Lothian, Grampian, Borders, Highlands and so on. These new regions are named after the months of the French revolutionary calendar: Vendémiaire, Brumaire, Frimaire, Nivôse, Pluviôse, Ventôse, Germinal, Floréal, Prairial, Messidor, Thermidor, Fructidor. The more northern the region, the more wintry the calendar name allocated.

SCOTLAND 57

The Scotland which has slipped under tundra permafrost and lies far to the north of the tree-line.

SCOTLAND 40

You're on the A725 heading south from Glasgow. You'll soon come to a fork in the road. Take the right hand route towards Stewartfield. At the next roundabout veer right onto the A726 for Paisley. Go through a series of roundabouts, passing a Holiday Inn on the right. Suddenly you'll be amongst dusty plains and curvy brutalist buildings, catalpa and eucalyptus trees. Welcome to East Kilbride!

When East and West Scotland were partitioned, Planner Smithson realised a new capital would be required for the Western Regions. Not just for administration, but to house the thousands of people displaced by the upheavals of the civil war. And so he commissioned Le Corbusier to design the New Town of East Kilbride from scratch as a city 'unfettered by the traditions of the past, a symbol of the nation's faith in the future'. Construction began in 1951, and by 1965 all but the futuristic Museum of Knowledge had been finished (the museum remains — like knowledge itself — incomplete to this day).

While not bound to please everyone, Corbu's characteristic 'Modular Brutalism' gives East Kilbride a fabulous monumentality, aided by the sculptural forms which don't so much dot the dusty, open landscape as dominate it with crushingly gargantuan symbols of peace, good will, and global harmony: an open hand, a dove, an eyeball, a hulking human form boiled in bronze. The place looks like a UNESCO office blown up to the scale of a city.

Looming beyond East Kilbride's empty squares stand Scotland's High Court, its Legislative Assembly, and the imposing hall of the Secretariat.

East Kilbride shares something with Brasilia, with Dhaka, with Chandigarh in the Punjab, and with the Pan African Parliament. In the relative poverty of Scotland, Le Corbusier was able to achieve what no rich country dared afford him: a blank slate, a year zero, endless confidence in his vision, and enormous resources. He responded by gifting Scotland with the world's most brutally optimistic and uplifting Modernist utopia.

Every utopia has its banana skin, of course. Here in East Kilbride, state employees ride the enormous distances from their gargantuan apartments to their monstrous offices on bicycles. At either end of the journey, the roofs leak; the French engineers failed to include the ceaseless precipitation of the Scottish climate in their calculations. Crows and starlings inhabit the parks intended as leisure quotas for the residents of the *unités d'habitation*. No one plays tennis in the courts provided.

But few are discouraged by East Kilbride's failings. If anything, they add an endearing fallibility to a city which would otherwise be too grid-like, too perfect, nothing but poured concrete, primary colours, and the International Style. Just when this monumental Scottish city – built, it seems, for peaceful giants – makes you think you're stuck in Tati's *Playtime*, you're reminded that it's also Moonbase Alpha.

SCOTLAND 58

The Scotland which achieves victory over its enemy, the sun, with costume design by Kazimir Malevich.

SCOTLAND 60

The Scotland pulsing with the rhythms of *The Rite of Spring*.

SCOTLAND 76

The mist-filled Scotland in which people chant Hugh MacDiarmid poems over Side Two of David Bowie's *Low*.

SCOTLAND 35

The Scotland in which you're not allowed to own more property than will fit into a rucksack.

SCOTLAND 154

INTERVIEWER They burnt your house?
SCOT Yes.
INTERVIEWER Why?
SCOT Because we were Scots. No other reason.
INTERVIEWER Where did you go?
SCOT They picked us up on the road as we were trying to escape, and put us on buses.
INTERVIEWER Who were *they*?
SCOT We were pretty sure who they were. They were the Irish, the same ones who burned our villages. They took us to a zone already under Irish control. It was a caravan park up in the mountains. I'll never forget the kids there... throwing stones up at the bus windows, spitting on us, cursing us, insulting our women.
INTERVIEWER Why did they hate you?
SCOT Because we were Scots. Filth, in their eyes. And easy prey. Any idiot could get a hard man reputation by abusing us. There was nothing we could do.
INTERVIEWER And then?
SCOT They blindfolded us and drove us a long way. For hours. We didn't know where we were going. We all had the same thought in our heads: that at the end of the road there would be a forest clearing, and a few shots

	from a pistol, and that would be it.
INTERVIEWER	They would execute you?
SCOT	Of course! What else? We were Scots. That was enough.
INTERVIEWER	After burning your houses and driving you so far? Why not do it there, in your village?
SCOT	I don't know – maybe they had professional executioners, beyond the reach of the law. Remember that at that point they were in league with the Welsh.
INTERVIEWER	Did you know where you were?
SCOT	We weren't in Scotland any more, we knew that. We all feared the same thing; that they had taken us to Wales.
INTERVIEWER	Why did you fear that?
SCOT	The Welsh – we had heard about them. A people without mercy. A people who hated the Scots even more than the Irish did. A race who would hack us to bits with the greatest of pleasure. If we were in Wales, we were lost.
INTERVIEWER	And were you?
SCOT	As soon as my blindfold was removed, I looked about. I could see bare hills, a small church, the distinctive gantry of a minehead. My heart sank. And that's when I heard the male voice choir.
INTERVIEWER	You heard a choir?
SCOT	Mostly tenors and basses. All men. Our blood turned to ice in our veins. Where else

	could we be than Wales? We were done, finished, ended.
INTERVIEWER	But then…?
SCOT	The choir got closer and closer. The shapes became men, and the men had faces, and the faces were smiling. Big, strong men grabbed us and held us shoulder high. The Welsh had changed sides. Everything we'd been told had been wrong, outmoded, stupid slander. These great-hearted Welshmen were our friends! We were safe!
INTERVIEWER	How did that make you feel?
SCOT	The way I still feel today. We owe everything to our comrades, the Welsh. They saved our lives. If they rule Scotland now they deserve nothing less. They have saved us just as they saved our land.

SCOTLAND 91

The Scotland in which roads are overgrown with vegetation and people hike along public footpaths.

SCOTLAND 121

The Scotland in which Prospero plays Ariel off against Caliban.

SCOTLAND 131

The Scotland in which forests move about, fulfilling an ancient prophecy.

SCOTLAND 81

The Scotland which has exchanged homelands with Denmark.

SCOTLAND 31

It's easy to see why Tricksy, the son of a Jamaican sailor wrecked on Orkney, felt so alienated growing up in Hamnavoe. The residents of the picturesque town – basically one long seafront, and the port for the Scrabster ferry – are massively white, and Hamnavoe's culture is one of the most monolithic in the British Isles. Cold weather and chronic alcoholism combine to give the town a strong sense of self-pity.

It was while Tricksy was down south in Edinburgh studying literature that he found his 'inner Orcadian'. Encountering the works of Bacon, Beckett and Burroughs, Tricksy was overwhelmed by the negativity and despair built into Modernist art.

'All the sick writers and anti-artists', he wrote in an early letter to Martina Topley-Bride, 'their works are the symptoms of a deep and (it may be) incurable malaise. Even with the songs of a talented group like The Specials, you ask yourself over and over again:

What does this come out of? What is Terry Hall trying to say?'

The nihilism of the work made Tricksy see his native Orkney with new eyes, and soon a locally rooted poetry began to flow forth from him. The distinctive Tricksyese language emerged first on a track called 'Shipping Forecast'. Over odd, stilted beats, strangled synthesizers, Smashing Pumpkins samples and the bray of a donkey, Tricksy intoned darkly:

The General Synopsis at 1300
Cold front Fair Isle to Shannon expected
South Utsire to Lundy by 1300 tomorrow
Atlantic high moving northeast expected 300 miles west
of Shannon 1036 by same time
High Humber 1029 losing its identity

Tricksy abandoned his PhD and returned to Hamnavoe, sustaining himself by writing a weekly column for *The Orcadian*. Before long he was also DJing regularly with a local posse who called themselves The Incredible Seven. Led by radio ham Marco Leonardi (a member of Orkney's Italian population, descended from prisoners of war interned on the island), The Incredible Seven later changed their name to Passive Attack. Tricksy stayed with the group for two albums before going solo.

If Orkney is monolithic it's also, of course, paleolithic. It was at the Bay of Skaill, on the windswept west coast of the Orcadian mainland, that Tricksy – filming the video for his 1994 song 'Overdone (Karmacobra)' – discovered one of Scotland's most impressive troves of buried treasure. The two rented helicopters were grounded and the video production became, momentarily, an archeological dig when Martina Topley-Bride uncovered first one silver piece, then another, and finally over a hundred ancient coins in the sand.

The precious hoard was stored in nearby Skaill House, once the home of Captain Cook. Here, in an unscripted improvisation, Tricksy was filmed squatting over the silver like a malicious crossdressing goblin, caressing the treasure while lipsynching his fragmented lyrics. After serving as props in the video, the coins were turned over to the Scottish government, which thanked Tricksy and Topley-Bride by giving them the key to the town of Thurso.

The 'Overdone (Karmacobra)' video also featured – dangling from helicopters by wire ropes – a sculpture by Japanese artist Masako Tori, rumoured to be romantically entangled with Tricksy at the time. Tori, the niece of one of Tokyo's richest property developers, had become deeply interested in Celtic lore, and had come to Orkney to photograph the standing stones at Stenness. The mysterious rocks later appeared as 'spacecraft for the dead' in her installation *Bom Na H-iu*.

Tricksy was rewarded by seeing his version of 'Karmacobra' outsell Passive Attack's three-to-one. His *Shipping Forecast* album went triple-platinum, allowing Tricksy to purchase Skaill House, where he still lives.

SCOTLAND 141

The Scotland from which half the population has emigrated to Madagascar, the other half to Israel.

SCOTLAND 73

Would the last to leave Scotland please switch off the light?

SCOTLAND 28

We were making a family trip to the town of Dunbar. My father drove the vintage Bentley. Pointing it in the general direction of the east coast, he avoided the crowded A199 corridor and stuck, instead, to green lanes between knolls where we'd encounter only the occasional tractor or flock of sheep. His penis took up so much space – bundled like a gaudy pink and blue scarf over his shoulder and folded in layers on the back seat – that Luisa and I had to sit in the front, one on top of the other.

My father's monologue was as circuitous as the route he had chosen, but certain themes recurred. One was the joy of having a penis as vast as his own.

'The penis is mightier than the sword,' he informed us, and sang in quivering baritone a snatch of advertising from the 19th century:

They come as a Boon and a Blessing to men
The Pickwick, the Owl, and the Waverley Pen.

Sexual pleasure, he informed us, was just like those pens – a boon and a blessing to mankind (which included womankind). Orgasm – however procured – was the greatest achievement of our species. 'Never be ashamed of phallic values,' he said. 'Two thousand years ago, when our ancestors lived on this coast in rough wattle cottages, forts and castles, and fought the Norsemen who came to rape and pillage, life was worse in almost every way. The sword had not yet given way to the penis.'

'But surely rape and pillage are the perfect penis values?' I challenged.

My father looked annoyed. 'I am not talking about the penises of others,' he said. 'It is our own penis which must prevail. When that happens, the Golden Age will be attained.'

We were skirting the coast now, and on our left the sea stretched blue and white to the horizon, framed by sky and gorse. I imagined Norsemen arriving from Norway in longships with ferocious faces carved into the prows, Norsemen who planned to burn Dunbar to the ground and inject their DNA into the local women. And from that DNA would eventually spring monsters like Dad.

'Those people in far distant millennia knew orgasm just as we do. Perhaps they lay fucking on this very harbour wall,' said my father, tugging on the handbrake and packing his penis into a rucksack while Luisa and I lugged the picnic hamper out of the boot.

'Of course they had a robust pagan religion which put the important things – the sun, the seasons, crops, community rituals and fertility – at the centre of everything.'

We spread a blanket out near the lighthouse and settled down to eat. As gulls wheeled overhead, scanning us with beaded eyes, my father pulled from the rucksack's outer pocket his well-worn copy of *Copulating Gorillas at Longinch*, a collection of poems by his old enemy Scotty Morocco. It was an ingrained habit of his to tear these poems apart at every opportunity.

'Read this,' said my father, stabbing at a passage and handing me the shabby book. He began to cut slabby sandwiches – white Milanda bread filled with a pink layer of processed salmon paste – into neat triangles.

While Luisa poured tea from a thermos flask, I read, for the umpteenth time, from the collection's title poem:

Picking at ticks and fleas he's no ape Valentino,
Is he?
It's a scene that Sartre could have used to show
Domestic misery.
She's not much better, wearing slippers, all unwanted
Intimacy;
Bald arse sagging like a sack, a fat ape slag,
Isn't she?

'It's so, so bad,' chuckled my father, shaking his head. 'Go on!'

He licks her hairy tits forensically, she cups his balls then
Gradually,
He licks then fucks her (sooner him than me!)
up the filthy rear, and
Frenziedly
Ejaculates, while all the while the monkeys clap
(The fucks)
Enthusiastically.

'Now,' said my father, stuffing his mouth with white and pink food and washing it down with a swig of tea, 'tell me what's wrong with that poem. Eh?'

'It's obscene?' I ventured.

'No, that's the best thing about it!' roared my father. 'Didn't you learn anything last time? Try again.'

'What's wrong is just that it's a poem by Scotty Morocco and Dad hates Scotty,' interjected Luisa, cattily.

'Shut up!' Dad bellowed.

'Is it the scansion?' I ventured, trying to remember what answer had placated him last time. 'Bad scansion?'

'Nothing to do with the form,' said my father, chomping on Milanda.

'I know, monkeys are not apes!' I cried.

'No, it's not that!'

'What's wrong with it, then?'

'I'll tell you what's wrong with it,' said Dad. 'The whole bloody attitude behind it, that's what. Examine the presuppositions! The hatred for sex! The disdain for orgasm! It's full of hate, hate for life.'

'I suppose it is,' I said.

SCOTLAND 138

In any natural process, there is a tendency for useful energy to dissipate. It is a peculiarity of Scotland's, however, that in that land this is not the case.

We shall not dwell here upon how this anomaly came to be, simply repeat that in Scotland, the entropy which affects all other systems in all other parts of the world does not apply.

In fact, rather than dissipating, useful energy in Scotland accumulates. Things grow more efficient over time. Systems which at first do not work well improve continuously. Disorder is perpetually decreasing.

This has made the Scots into lazy slatterns, for only the smallest amount of effort and organisation is required to set in motion the process known as 'The Bravery' – quite the opposite of entropy.

Left to their own devices, the natural forces of time and The Bravery inevitably improve everything that happens in Scotland. Every arrow, no matter how stray when fired, hits the bull's eye. Things become cheaper and yet quality improves – a principle known elsewhere only in relation to the price-to-performance ratio of computers. There are no cleaners, because things tend to become tidier over time.

If a Scot looks as dishevelled as Einstein when he leaves the house in the morning, he will return in the evening looking as smart as Newton. Every clumsy movement will prove presciently deft.

If a Scot starts old and wrinkled, he will end young and

smooth, with taut, well-formed features. If he begins fat and out of shape, he will become steadily more trim, fit and lithe as time passes. If he is weak and close to death, he will, before long, be strapping and strong.

There's no friction, so all of Scotland's transport runs like a Maglev train, but without magnets. No machine requires fuel in Scotland; they all run by perpetual motion, perfectly self-contained. The more you move your body, the more energy you have to move it.

As a result, Scotland has become the workshop of the world, and a prime tourist destination too. Most places, no matter how relaxing, sap you of energy. But the more time you spend in Scotland, the more energy you have. Holidays have to be forcibly curtailed, otherwise visitors would stay forever. The Scottish tourist visa is a strict three weeks.

Not all effects of The Bravery are positive. You know the expression 'butter wouldn't melt in her mouth'? Well, in Scotland it doesn't. Ice doesn't melt in a glass of whisky, either. Digestion proves extraordinarily difficult because nothing breaks down. And nobody can sleep because, as the day wears on, a resident of Scotland grows less and less tired.

In Scotland, all noise turns into music, and all music becomes increasingly harmonious. Notes never decay, but hang in the air, getting stronger and longer. It's unbearable, actually.

Because there is no waste, there's a kind of pervasive selfishness in Scotland. Things don't release the excess energy on which other things can feed. There are no parasites, no niche life forms, no chains of dependency, no harmonious ecosystems. There are only massively efficient, self-sufficient machines which hog their own energy forever, like hot water bottles that never get cold, but never warm you either.

These anomalies of physics have been Scotland's undoing. Nation after nation has attacked, seeking to harness The Bravery and use it for their own ends. Fortunately, even if the Scots begin by losing these wars, they end up winning them decisively. So nobody has yet succeeded in defeating them or capturing The Bravery.

If outsiders did capture it, they would soon discover the disadvantages. Nobody would ever die again! Every struck note would become a stuck note! The world would be in hell!

So far, the Scots have been courageous enough to keep The Bravery to themselves. And every day they grow more courageous still.

SCOTLAND 111

The Scotland which reverts to patronymics, in the Norse style: where Jarem Robertson is the father of Hercules Jaremson, who is the father of John Herculesson, who sires William Johnsson, who marries Margaret Jarmsdochter and produces Hercules Williamson in Muckle Roe.

SCOTLAND 104

The Scotland in which cities are broken up and the entire population lives on the land, in equidistant crofter's cottages.

SCOTLAND 61

The Scotland divided up into a graph-paper-like grid, with one town at the centre of each square and one square at the centre of each town.

SCOTLAND 144

Scotland's return to puritanism could so easily have been based on its own history; John Knox, the Plymouth Brethren, Calvinism. It could even have been a response to Islamic neo-fundamentalism. Instead, it arrived thanks to evangelical entrepreneur Brent Shouter.

Shouter's donations to the nationalists officially came with no strings attached, but unofficially made him Scotland's moral puppeteer. If he wanted neo-puritanism, well, that's what Scotland would get.

Since no really modern traditions of puritanism existed, a synthetic concoction would have to be assembled. There were, of course, things resembling puritanism in left-wing traditions like feminism and environmentalism, but Shouter wanted no truck with such radicalism. The puritanism he required had to be a conservative one. There could be no question, though, of learning anything from Saudi Arabia.

And so Shouter turned to the Shakers. Whereas Scottish cities were once rebuilt as pastiches of Charles Rennie Mackintosh surrounded by brutal industrial high-rises, they were now redeveloped in the style of Shaker communities. I say 'style' advisedly; Shouter did not believe in the communism of Shaker social structure or work relations. What he liked was the unadorned simplicity of their styles of architecture, the plainness, cleanliness and practicality which was their hallmark.

Shouter organised a series of blockbuster exhibitions on Shaker style. He also launched Shakestation, a heavily subsidised, heavily advertised furniture warehouse specialising in affordable Shaker furniture for the masses. Soon Ikea was completely routed, and closed its last Scottish store.

As homes were transformed by Shakestation furniture, the Scots found a new spirituality infusing their daily lives. Chairs were hung on hooks mounted high on simple wooden walls when not in use, televisions and radios disappeared, and people disconnected from the Internet, preferring to sing Shaker songs around a log fire. Circular workshops were built in gardens where men manipulated simple woodworking tools, wearing grey tunics, aprons and shoulder-length hair cut halfway down the forehead in a bang.

Women, mostly celibate and segregated, worked at needlework samplers bearing edifying messages. They cooked, cleaned, sang, and spoke in tongues. There were ceremonies all across Scotland involving the laying-on of hands, and miracles became commonplace in the land; it was said that true believers could see water rushing up from the ground to heaven.

The Shouter-Shakerification of Scotland increased national longevity by several years, but decreased the nation's birthrate. As Shouter himself became an old man, bereft of any direct heirs who shared his beliefs, it grew clear that the current order would have to change if Scotland were to survive.

But how to reach the Scots? They had by and large detached themselves from all known media and all existing towns, preferring to wait in self-sustaining rural communities for the second coming of an androgynous Christ.

It was this Second Coming which provided the government with a way to recapture Scotland. A fake Christ was prepared – one who fitted the Shakers' specifications exactly.

By the time this Government Christ had become the leader of the Shouter-Shakers, and led them back to the abandoned cities, telling them it was His Plan that they should live there and work and multiply, Brent Shouter was dead.

Denounced by the Government Christ, Shouter's memory was condemned by the Shaker sect he had created. His embalmed body, resting in a simple tomb atop a mountain in Perthshire, was stolen one evening and vanished without a trace.

SCOTLAND 65

The Scotland whose main exports are reggae dub plates and ingots of pig iron.

SCOTLAND 90

The Scotland in which human voices wake us, and we drown.

SCOTLAND 22

The Scotland so heartily reforested that it even exceeds Japan's 70% forest cover, attracting the return of bears and beavers in numbers that have not been seen since the need to defeat the Spanish Armada induced the Scots to chop down their Scots Pines – the *Pinus sylvestris* you're now more likely to see at the Sea of Okhotsk than in Scotland.

SCOTLAND 106

The Scotland which lies sunken under five metres of water without ceasing to go about its business.

SCOTLAND 137

When David Bowie was calling himself the 'Führerling' in his 1970s interviews, most people took the declaration that he would make a great fascist leader of Britain with a pinch of salt, or some other white powder. But Scotland took him seriously, and by 1980 he was firmly established in power in our land. The main result, as I recall, is that we were all forced to wear baggy 'Bowie trousers', emphasise our cheekbones, and tease our hair into New Romantic styles featuring blond highlights. Following the release of his disappointing *Tonight* album, however, Bowie's Gleneagles HQ was the target of a swift and decisive military coup. Since then, singers have been explicitly forbidden to run countries, and trousers tend to be tighter.

SCOTLAND 56

You reach this Scotland after a restless night in an intercity coach. It's exciting to be here, because it's so much bigger and more diverse than the place you come from. Gazing through the coach window with grey-pouched eyes, you see people of all races, shapes and sizes. Asians, Africans, Russians, Arabs, Peruvians; they're all here in Scotland, a world in microcosm.

But there's something depressing about this place. Enormous, flimsy buildings in indeterminate styles – half-timbered, gothic, imperial – line the edges of broad, polluted streets full of aggressive traffic. The clouds hang low, each one harbouring a landing airliner. Everything is shabby, fit for purpose and nothing more. It will all be cleared away with bulldozers shortly and replaced by something equally ugly, and nobody will care.

The ethnic communities living here don't seem to see the ugliness of it; in fact, the interiors you glimpse from the coach window are replicas of environments from the other side of the world. These are immigrants from space, living in a dream which protects them, clinging to their customs and costumes, nestling tight with their families, working hard for money. You hear their music – informed by nostalgia and suffering – spilling out from behind bead curtains. You smell the tang of their cuisine, the unfamiliar spices of their street markets, their shabby warehouses filled with boxes, polystyrene padding, and coat hangers.

Police cars and ambulances in acid shades of yellow and blue overtake the coach, their sirens howling in strange electronic patterns. Nobody seems to notice; life goes on in the vast car parks surrounding hypermarkets which sell plants, DIY equipment, self-storage, computers, carpets and office furniture. Newspaper billboards flash populist, conservative headlines. You glimpse red plush corner pubs, see men lingering around the wells of staircases and on the corners of streets. Habit and conformity blind passers-by to the threat of petty crime.

Approaching the enormous capital city of Scotland – the capital of the world, some call it – you feel pretty much the way you imagine its immigrants do. You resent the imperial power this place has over your more modest land, and what you know of the history of your two nations disgusts and ashames you. You and everyone you love have been treated like scum by these people!

Yet you can't deny that you're also attracted by this extraordinary megalopolis, the capital of Scotland – by its wealth and power and fame. You feel your aggression becoming mere passive aggression, then compliance. In your mind's eye, the pages of a calendar peel away. You'll come here temporarily, then repeatedly, then stay, and before you know it you'll be old and have been here all your life – a servant of empire, another cog in the Babylonian machinery.

You remember the summer job you had back home, working alongside a fellow countryman who spent forty years in Scotland before returning home. When you told him you were thinking of coming here to work, he said: 'Don't do it, son. You'll waste your life as I wasted mine. Scotland will eat up your soul and take all your energy. That place only cares for one thing: money. And there's so much more to life than that.'

He's right – you feel a bit sick already, just trying to breathe the thick, toxic air here – but somehow you know that this mass of global millions, all attracted by the same thing that brought you here, will make all sorts of stories possible in your life, stories that couldn't happen in the small, racially monolithic place you're from. On balance, you want to risk it. You want to discover whether you can make it here, amongst these ugly imperial buildings. You too want your chance to be devoured by this vast, famous, callous monster, the capital of Scotland.

SCOTLAND 165

The Scotland in which all the films star flowers and thistles. Human actors are supporting players to the flowers and thistles. The message: if we try hard enough, we too might become flowers and thistles.

SCOTLAND 12

The Scotland in which Scotland 'is an alternative editing table for reality, and its major political task consists of showing how precarious our so-called "natural" context is'.

SCOTLAND 124

On a superficial level, Scottish cities look like cities anywhere. Their parks look like parks, their trains like trains, and so on. Nevertheless, this 'likeness' is an illusion. When we look at, board, and ride a train in Scotland it would be foolish to see it as anything like a normal train. It only looks like a train: in fact, it's a set of Scottish etiquettes and assumptions travelling through space.

Yesterday I took one of Edinburgh's beautiful new trams from Pilton to Restalrig. I was standing in the first car, right behind the driver. I noticed a series of odd cries, muffled by glass, and realised they were coming from the white-gloved driver himself. Alone in his cabin, he was accompanying his actions with sharp cries. It was astonishing, yet I was the only passenger paying any attention.

My first thought was that the driver was mentally ill. I admired the tram company's lack of prejudice in giving such a responsible job to someone with Tourette's Syndrome, but worried for our safety. Then I remembered that autistic people are often highly talented in narrowly defined areas; drawing buildings, for instance, or memorizing music. Perhaps this man was an excellent driver, better than someone mentally continent.

I watched – and filmed – the lunatic. He did seem exceptionally focused. At each station he made a series of florid manual curlicues, approximating the gestures of an orchestral conductor. He pointed vigorously at the TV screens in his console displaying the doors, then pulled the tram away from the station with both gloved hands on the accelerator lever, uttering as if by compulsion the ecstatic, falling cry: '*Kkkkyyyyyoooooooooo!*'

Crossing points or passing other trams, he made similar noises. They seemed less like words than explosions of passion for the regular events of his job. It was a passion as formalised as the whoops and howls of Highland Fling dancers.

More speculations rattled through my mind. Was this a trainee driver, taught to call out loud the actions he was making in the same way that, as a learner driver, I'd been taught to say 'mirror, signal, manœuvre'? I began to see, beside the driver in the cabin, the lineaments of a ghostly 'guru driver', a calm, modest yet deeply authoritative 'master of the tram'. This trainee, I speculated, was addressing his internalised 'tram master', and calling out the beloved gestures entailed by his duties, with passionate capitulation.

Later, a Scottish friend told me that such weird behaviour is normal here. All tram drivers shout out their actions in this way, not just trainees.

It seemed impossible to see this driver as (in the usual cant) 'a man who just happens, at this moment, to be driving a tram... but who could be so much more than that if he wanted to be!' Individualistic societies cover their hierarchical verticality with the ideology of 'equality of opportunity' (which of course entails its less benign cousin, inequality of result).

But Scottish society is superflat, diffuse. Ultimate value might exist at any point on the horizontal plane. Everybody is as important as everybody else, everybody bows to everybody else. Capitulation is mutual, investment total.

Individualistic societies prefer us to be divided, to wear masks, to adopt a casual, rather non-committal attitude to our jobs. Only select occupations (entrepreneur, artist, designer, sexual pervert) are really vocational in a passionate way. A tram driver in such a maverick, opportunistic society might make us feel indifference, scorn, pity – make us hope, at the very least, that a nice family and hobbies compensate for the uninteresting drudgery of his job.

But this employee seemed to have the very soul of a tram driver. I was overwhelmed by admiration and jealousy. This man had made his occupation his religion. Completely without vanity, he was his own ideal.

I wanted his commitment, his dignity. I wanted to wear white gloves and make delicate ceremonial gestures even while doing something completely pragmatic and down-to-earth. I wanted to cry out in ecstasy each time we trundled over a crossing. Reborn as this tram driver, I would never feel unimportant. In fact, I would feel like a star. I would catch glimpses of fascination and envy from children and adults alike.

I'd never be surprised to find myself being photographed or filmed. It would seem perfectly natural that video game arcades featured simulations of my job. My glamour would be apparent, though lightly worn. I would hand over to the next driver with a low bow and a deep sense of satisfaction – not to have the job behind me, but to have the same glories ahead of me tomorrow, and the day after, and forever. Whatever I was paid would be okay. My reward would be a deep sense of legitimacy. Superlegitimacy, in fact.

My job would only look like tram driving. In fact, it would be something tremendously Scottish: a sense of almost fanatical dedication, a capitulation of self to social role, an internalisation of social requirements, a going-to-extremes, an etiquette, a sense of honour. Hugh MacDiarmid's father, reluctant to see his son become a poet, said: 'Very well, if you become a poet, at least become Scotland's best.' That's how I would approach my job too. For satisfaction does not consist in evading, avoiding, denying or escaping your social role, but in embracing it completely, joyfully.

By limiting myself, I have set myself free.

My wife refers to me as 'Mr Tram Driver' even in bed. I wear my uniform even on days when I have no work, as the schoolgirls here do, so wrapped up in the deep joy and honour of being a schoolgirl, the pleasures and freedoms of what some would see as a categorical limitation, is revealed in Scotland as a categorical liberation – liberation *into* category rather than out of it.

We arrive at Restalrig, our terminus. The last passenger disembarks, and I park and lock the beloved tram. As I walk along the shore in my dark blue uniform, I'm sure I hear someone – probably the sea itself – call out a cheerful greeting: 'Thank you for your great work, Mr Tram Driver!' Smiling, I touch two white-gloved fingers to the skip of my cap.

SCOTLAND 145

The Scotland in which there is no repetition. No two houses are alike, nobody has the same name as anybody else, there are no habits. Every television show is seen just once, and no Web site visited twice. If you've used a word before, you have to make up a new one.

SCOTLAND 126

The Scotland in which you can make children into little masterpieces by taking them out of circulation and bringing them up 'strange'.

SCOTLAND 113

The Scotland in which Holyrood has become Bollyrood; Indian film producers, ravished by our sweeping mountainsides and cascading waterfalls, have purchased the nation in order to use it as a backdrop for their highly successful romantic musical comedies. The misty Highlands are now filled with duetting, pirouetting Indian couples, the parliament is a production facility, and the Palace of Holyroodhouse a sound stage.

SCOTLAND 155

The Scotland in which independence has led to withdrawal from the European Union and a choice for citizens: a Scottish passport or a European one? Berlin and Barcelona or Ballantrae and Braemar?

SCOTLAND 44

The Scotland in which the national anthem is Joseph Beuys and Henning Christiansen's *Schottische Symphonie aus Celtic*, recorded at the Edinburgh College of Art on August 21st, 1970.

SCOTLAND 105

The Scotland of the Munro Mao, whose Long March takes him over two hundred and eighty-four mountains.

SCOTLAND 79

The Scotland which gets as rich – and as dull – as Monaco.

SCOTLAND 147

The Scotland which realises its breasts are bare and stretches an enormous bra from Banff to Applecross.

SCOTLAND 33

Edinburgh's avenues, vacant and impersonal, shining in the rain with neon mantras – Tennant's, Tunnock's, Menzies – are as inflexible as the Ten Commandments. The winding side streets, human-scaled and friendly, punctuated by the pink and white glow of soft drink machines and Peace on Earth posts, are pagan, practical, haphazard, medieval; agglutinations of habit and custom which work because people know them.

As long as they aren't foreigners.

Paying the taxi and pulling my red suitcase up the wynd, I feel like an outsider. As I climb to the fourth floor of the ziggurat-roofed apartment block, I realise that my scale is all wrong. The stairs are claustrophobically narrow and the flat at the top is like a doll's house.

Helen shows me around. The bathroom is a single moulded piece of plastic, the bath a mere slot, the bedroom a mat behind a sliding door.

I remove my shoes and greet Viv, Helen's roommate. She's beautiful and, as we sip soup and eat fish fingers off an electric hotplate which takes up the whole table, she shows me books written by her friend Dr Fulton, a TV comedian who has a nightly show. His latest work is about masturbation: under chapter headings decorated with humorous, friendly little penises, Fulton discusses early wanking rituals with big names from the world of Scottish showbiz, like Rab C. Nesbitt. It's hard to imagine an American parallel: Conan's Guide to Onan, perhaps?

Viv informs me that Fulton is a once-a-day man. How often do I do it, she enquires? Well, I'm not as young as I used to be, I tell her, but once a day sounds reasonable. It's a perfectly practical question to ask a guest. We'll all be sleeping in the same bed.

The girls have rented a two video set of the 1979 Ray Bradbury epic *The Martian Chronicles*. Before jet lag carries me off to the box bed, I watch a poignant episode. Some astronauts arrive on Mars to discover why colleagues from earlier missions have gone silent. They climb out of their spacecraft to discover, not red soil and craters, but an idyllic scene of green and white; picket fences, leafy trees and church spires. It's the Illinois town where the mission captain grew up.

The captain's quickly surrounded by reassuring figures from his childhood – his dead brother, his Ma and Pa, his first prom date. They feed him chocolate cake and the prom date takes the astronaut outside for a kiss. He goes to sleep in an exact replica of the family house, his brother in the next bed. Only when he decides he should return to the ship to radio a report back to Earth does his brother reveal that he and the whole cast of this little scene are Martians. It's all been an illusion, a seductive stage-set built by telepathy in the mind of each astronaut. These mind games were the only defence the Martians could mount against invaders from a planet with superior weapons.

Scottish people are Martian too. Like the long-robed inhabitants of the red planet in the Ray Bradbury movie, they're constantly struggling against invasion by barbarian foreigners, outsiders with inferior culture but superior fire power. Like the Martians, the Scots resort to subtle mental seduction rather than outright combat. They get into your mind, charming it with familiar scenes made only slightly strange by the thin Martian air. The great capital city of their planet, Edinburgh – in reality a grim sprawl of concrete boxes – becomes a succession of fantastical shapes straight out of Robert Louis Stevenson: castles, volcanoes, spectral monuments, lamplit closes.

The next day I walk from the Grassmarket to South Bridge with Helen and Viv, shopping for a bike. There's a craze for folding models with little wheels. I find an orange one on the Pleasance for £120, and wheel it through streets choc-a-bloc with 'sky people'.

In the criss-cross mesh of streets, Scottish teenagers sit around under small trees. Girls rule here, whether in short swinging tartan skirts and loose socks or neo-hippy tie dye. There's an art school with open studios – mostly pleasant fluff – and a charmed back garden. It's all Jamaican paintwork and crazy scaffolding outside, inside tiny rooms you have to stoop to enter. The tone is gentle, creative, curious. The kids who pass by in pairs are fey, shy, weird, friendly looking, laid-back. Martians, all right.

SCOTLAND 49

The Scotland which deliberately bombs itself back to the Stone Age so that all its products become relics as priceless as the ones on display at the National Museum of Scotland, Chambers Street.

SCOTLAND 80

The Scotland in which the Edinburgh Festival runs all year, and in every city.

SCOTLAND 152

The Scotland which becomes the first nation in the world to outlaw cars.

SCOTLAND 85

The Scotland in which a gigantic statue in the Tay Estuary holds aloft a torch which burns both night and day, welcoming the poor of the world – and as a result, will soon be rich.

SCOTLAND 15

The tremendously powerful Scotland which nano-technology has made, by and large, too small to see.

SCOTLAND 63

Fulton, Viv's friend the famous television comedian, has invited us to dinner at his house in Marchmont, a studenty area famous for golf links and secondhand bookstores.

We take the number 6. The house is on a bustling side street. Fulton has built it himself. It's an elegant four-floored concrete box. In the basement there's a library, on the first floor a big kitchen, and above, sleeping quarters and the roof.

Fulton's manservant wears shades. He prepares our supper: raw salmon and sliced turnip in plastic boxes, deliciously fresh and tender. Fulton arrives presently with his writer friend Jim Usher. They're an ebullient pair of comedy musclemen. Tomorrow they're heading off for a holiday in Bratislava 'because the girls there cost only a tenner!' They're joking, of course. Fulton does a live TV show every day, and Easter is one of his few chances to take a holiday.

The conversation quickly turns to sex. Usher, heavily tattooed, thick-lipped and likeable, tells us he loves nothing more than drinking girls' pee. It's the best way to absorb the essence of a woman. Usher has spent time in jail for drug possession, and his latest books on drugs and Russia have been bestsellers. He's an important chapter in Fulton's masturbation book. Fulton has also spent time in the clink; on a tour of the US he presented a highway patrol cop with a fake driving licence. He shows us the absurd document: it features a photo of Fulton in an afro wig, Fulton with Inversneckie eyebrows.

Fulton and Usher present themselves as perverted wildmen, full of the unabashed enthusiasm of the geek. The assembled company listens to their anecdotes without the slightest trace of alarm. At the end of the evening, Fulton, like a sentimental laird, promises me safe passage in the world of Scottish showbiz. 'You are a foreigner,' he tells me, 'but I like outsiders.'

There's a strong Amsterdam feel to Stockbridge. That's where, as evening falls, I meet Shirley Manson and Sharleen Spiteri at the Cozi Bar and Grill. Obey the Giant posters designate this a site of international subcultural importance. Two Friends With You mannequins guard the door like the demons at the entrance to a Buddhist temple.

Inside there's already a crowd of creative-looking people. A middle-aged Japanese fashionista-ballerina type sips an after-work dram with two Scottish assistants. She looks like an exiled Rei Kawakubo.

Stockbridge style is a more relaxed extension of the Pentlands vibe. This bar is a shrine to Boards of Canada, whose *Music Has the Right to Children* album sleeve, with its grotesque, bleached catalogue hippies – so 1970s, so Pentlands-retro! – is on the wall. The shell of the building is cheerfully shabby, but the café is full of kitsch art trinkets and expensive mid-century modern sofas.

I lounge on white vinyl with Shirley and Sharleen, who flatter me rotten all evening. We scrawl ideas on napkins, look at a frizzy-haired pre-raphaelite photoshoot Shirley did earlier today, plan records. Sharleen tells me Beck, recording his new album in a studio nearby, is expecting me to drop by at some point. Maybe I'll go tomorrow.

Pedalling my new orange bike at breakneck speed along the cherry blossom paths by the Water of Leith, I feel as happy as Peewee Herman. I'm Gainsbourg in *Anna* and *Slogan*, Shirley and Sharleen are my Birkin and Bardot. Stockbridge is Amsterdam, Stockbridge is Mars – you can tell by the canals.

The Scots are embracing me, the Scots are resisting me. Their portables are chiming with 'Lemon Incest'. They're fucking with my brain via telepathy. And I'm loving every Martian minute.

SCOTLAND 136

The Scotland which makes a Scotland shape in the centre of the European landmass, the same way Finland makes a Finland shape in Scandinavia.

SCOTLAND 20

The Scotland which, exactly ten years after the publication of my *Book of Scotlands*, sweeps me to power, Velvet Revolution style.

SCOTLAND 18

The Scotland of my dreams is Stirling University crossed with an enormous late night shopping centre, crossed with Chinatown. There are dim sum stands, 24-hour university bookshops, fleapit cinemas, warrens of wholesale clothing dealers, hothouses filled with rainforests, artificial spray and moss, priceless ruins integrated into shopping malls, branches of Habitat, underground monorail systems, arcades full of dive bars run by noise musicians, hot spring resorts resembling flooded museums, museums resembling ghost train rides, domed student centres, art-schools-turned-gentlemen's-clubs, mazes, zoos, madhouses, monasteries, theatres,

international government agencies in permanent session,
hidden rooms staging panel discussions, replicas of sci-fi
film sets, ruined areas cordoned off with police tape,
casinos, grottos, 1970s-style hotels for the *nomenklatura*,
health clubs, brothels, police headquarters, military
barracks, ant hills, Vietnamese warehouses, oil-scented
garages, science labs like the now demolished ones
at my old school, Nissen huts, small indoor airports
from which microlights take off and land through a
hole two metres in diameter, fallow fields containing
skeletal donkeys, floor upon floor of restaurants with
theatrical set designs, wedding receptions, chai wallahs,
funicular railways running up inside hollow mountains,
neglected folk museums staffed by volunteers, neolithic
roundhouses, laundromats, empty areas full of
fluorescent coin operated food machines, waiting rooms
with moulded chairs where Teletext tickers report sports
results, bowling alleys, flower shops, flea markets,
warehouses filled with bicycles reclaimed by the police,
fish processing factories, granary bins, poultry sheds on
an unimaginably vast scale, yellow chickens extending to
the horizon, internal seas, salt mines accessible via deep
lift shafts, asteroid craters on the moon's moons, sets
built for children's television programmes, radio studios,
garden allotments, kabuki theatres, boudoirs featuring
spinets, wax museums, cabinets of curiosities, pine
saunas scattered with sand, sculptors' studios along with
their naked models, greenhouses and garden decoration
superstores, carpet warehouses and cream tea cafeterias,

scone bakeries, nuclear power stations, reservoirs, dry docks and barnyards.

SCOTLAND 115

The Scotland entirely redecorated in the postmodern, 18th century style of Ian Hamilton Finlay's garden at Little Sparta. It's called, naturally, Big Sparta.

SCOTLAND 142

The Scotland in which we talk like The Broons and dress like Kenneth McKellar.

SCOTLAND 96

His execution was a fake – Saddam Hussein is alive and well and living in Scotland. He rules the nation from the Palace of Holyroodhouse, guarded by a massive monument shaped like two crossed scimitars.

SCOTLAND 13

You move your left-hand bishop's pawn to b3, a favourite opening. Scotland responds – with astonishing recklessness – by moving his queen's pawn to d5, opening his queen and king to attack.

You press your advantage, immediately moving your queen out diagonally to a4, and – just two moves into the game! – checking Scotland's king.

Scotland blocks your check with his knight, allowing you to move a pawn up from b2 to b4, alongside your queen. Normally Scotland would take your pawn immediately, but the check from your queen prevents him. Instead he moves his king's pawn up to e5. Now you threaten his check-blocking knight with the pawn, and the Scottish knight hops back to e7, protecting the black king.

The sun is setting behind h8.

You move your pawn another square forward, to within striking distance of his pawns. But they can't respond, because your queen's check is once more slanting directly at the King of Scotland. A black pawn blocks it, and you draw the first blood of the game, taking Scotland's pawn at a7.

There is a splash of silver water and some black smoke rises from the board.

Scotland moves his other knight into play, vaguely menacing a cavalier pincer strategy now that the two equestrians have been freed of their protective duties.

You must step up the pressure. You advance the pawn at

g2 to g4, intending to menace his knight at f6. But this is your first major misstep: you failed to notice that his bishop was aimed at your destination square. Your pawn is swiftly devoured by the diagonal ecclesiastic.

A chilling sound of giggling is coming from the region of the rusty garden gate.

Now the mitred and fearsome John Knox stands alone and vulnerable on your half of the board, protected by a distant knight. You threaten him with your bishop's pawn and he retreats.

You have the impression that someone is smiling under the ground.

Your bishop makes a bold sweep to g5, only to be menaced by a pawn. You retreat one diagonal square and the pawn moves forward, past you.

Numbers of pieces are coughing.

Intuition guides you to move your knight up to c4, from whence it can check the Scottish king, threatened only by the black queen, herself threatened now by your king's pawn. You execute this check, only to be blocked by the Scottish king himself, who veers protectively in front of his spouse.

There is blood on the teeth of a comb.

You move your own king forward to threaten his knight, but – disaster! – you have failed to notice that the beast is lined up to take your queen! The carnivorous monster makes quick work of her, snorting and pawing at the turf.

You would be able to think more clearly if you were not in love.

You are at a loss. If only you could dispose of his bishop, your knight – now in the thick of the Scottish enemy – could menace both queen and castle at once. But the Scottish king chooses this moment to slide out, preventing your plan and, what's more, exposing your invading knight to the menace of the black queen.

Suddenly you have the feeling that you have lived this scenario before, in every detail.

You move your king towards the Scottish monarch, hoping to give your pawn safe passage. The black knight swings forward. Your king edges toward the left edge, and the knight pounces on the abandoned pawn, checking you at the same time. You threaten him with your king and the Scottish bishop moves forward to protect him.

Dawn is breaking, and the blasted oaks are lined up against a strong titanium white.

When you were a child, you pinned a calendar stolen from an Italian fashion magazine to your wall.

The seamstress sits alone in her room and spins.

A ghost, opening the door, is caught on CCTV.

The game ends in a draw.

SCOTLAND 77

What a filthy, yeasty orifice is that place called Scotland! Better call it 'Twatland'. Everyone there is a woman, or dresses as one. Their hemlines are so high, Hadrian's Wall had to be raised to keep those Amazons from devouring the entire world with their lust.

Oh, Fellini's *City of Women* is nothing to Quintland, Twatland, Cutland! For a start, there is no Mastroianni romantic or mad enough to wander enchanted through its forests, its glens, its cities. No man is mad enough for it, and in Scotland, no men are permitted. The prohibition comes not from the Scottish Amazons themselves, but from the authorities of all the other countries in the world. They cannot afford to lose their men.

But, like swinish sirens, the Scottish women try their best to seduce. Oh, how they try! They wear white stilettos and the shortest possible of skirts, even in the coldest possible of weathers. Every night for them is Friday night, and every street is Lothian Road. Every bar is called The Pig in Knickers, and throbs with raucous, inane laughter and cheap boy band hits.

Every party at The Pig in Knickers is a hot hen party. Where once the sharp, manly tang of beery urine would have been expelled through Vent-Axia ventilators out onto the cobbled yards beyond, now an appalling, needy perfume – the alkaline scent of a hundred vaginal passages – wafts like a terrible warning.

Enter these dens at your peril! For your manhood

will be devoured alive, your genital organs severed within seconds by the milky *vagina dentata* every Scotswoman possesses!

See them stagger, wrapped in feathers, shrieking like birds, along the pier late at night! Some will fall in, but no matter, their enormous breasts will help them float. If they don't, there are more wenches where those came from! Pay no attention to the thrashing of the cold harbour water, the cries for help! Board the first ship you can find and pray that the crew, like you, are males in drag!

Oh, men go to Scotland, of course they do. They disguise themselves as women to get in, lured by the promise of endless sex with undiscriminating slatterns who have never seen a man and long to wrap flabby, greedy labia around the doric column of a solid, marbled penis.

But few men who have penetrated Scotland and splashed her mottled pink thighs with their slippery, eager sperm live to tell the tale. Those who do hobble through life in stunned silence, or gibber like monkeys, ceaselessly sniffing their damaged genitals and pawing at the burnt skin of their thighs. They fear and shun all women. Some enter monasteries, others are sold to zoos.

But even these deranged, destroyed apes have not entirely lost their reason. Point them in the direction of Scotland – Twatland, Cutland, Quintland – and they will start to screech and jabber, cling to your jacket, dart their eyes around in panic. Anywhere, they seem to say, anywhere but there! Do not push us back into that den of rabid hyenas! Do not thrust us into the sulphur of that infernal cut! Save us from Scotland, land of women!

SCOTLAND 93

The Scotland which revives Gaelic the way Israel revived Hebrew.

SCOTLAND 135

The Scotland assailed by rockets launched from England (the suburbs of Carlisle prove particularly aggressive).

SCOTLAND 161

The Scotland planted so thickly with brambles that you can't crawl anywhere without having your face and arms scratched to bits.

SCOTLAND 159

The Scotland in which every building is demolished and replaced by a Modernist white cube.

SCOTLAND 16

From the moment Scotland lifted all tax and regulatory oversight on its business and banking sector, it became a haven for people like me: successful wealth creators only hindered by scrutiny, mavericks too dynamic to be held back by the rules that govern others.

I arrived here this evening with Colin, a money launderer with a big red face and a white linen suit. We shared a Falcon 900B, with interior design by Marc Newson.

I must say, it's always good to get to Scotland. You sense a certain liberty, ease and deregulation as soon as you step out of the mini-jet; it hits you like a sirocco or a fine-misted drizzle.

Colin and I were whisked to Stageagles Spa, our retreat in the Campsies. I had my usual suite: a low-rise, multi-level complex with plasma walls of lily pads, a swimming pool, two gyms, a master bedroom featuring a donut-shaped bed wrapped around a fire pillar, and a 'rain terrace' where my *après sauna* sweat can be spotted away by the sensual finger-touches of soft Scottish rain.

An hour or so after checking in, when I had stripped to a towel and was sipping pink whisky, an identity parade of girls was sent up. I chose Morag, and the rest were dismissed. Scottish women have pale skin, lightly freckled – so different from the boiled, leathery red hides of our wives!

After Morag and I had made love on the donut's chestnut-scented water mattress, I gazed into the frosted glass of the fire pillar.

'Tell me a story,' I said. 'One of your Scottish myths or legends.'

While Morag recounted a charming tale of lairds, tartan, claymores, grouse, heather, potatoes and breweries, a dozen Scottish Country Dancing Lasses in their early teens slipped into the room and reeled around the fire pillar in slow motion. The effect was piquant, particularly as the pink whisky was starting to take hold.

Soon there was a commotion of heartily vulgar laughter and Colin – dressed only in a towel and red as a lobster – crashed in, accompanied by his girl, Senga.

The fine-skinned Scots wrapped around each other like smoke, or cats. 'Tell us about your lives back home,' they coaxed. 'Your business, your wives, your money.'

We said we didn't want to talk about that. We were here to relax, to escape, to enjoy ourselves! And of course, to do a little banking business.

The pink lights dimmed, and the Scottish Country Dancing Lasses slipped out unobtrusively. There would be an opportunity later to bid for one as a souvenir.

We asked about the surfing, the scuba-diving, and whether there'd been any earthquakes recently. While the girls told their inconsequential stories – nothing ever happens in Scotland – a team of Highland masseurs rubbed deep relaxation into our bodies with expert hands.

Alerted by electronic sensors to optimal rain conditions, the glass skylight above our heads slid back on its hydraulic struts and we delighted in a haze of drizzle which only heightened the pleasure of the massage. We each took a line of Scottish-grade cocaine mixed with crushed methaqualone.

After half an hour we ordered some more pink whisky and a fresh set of girls. While they were on the way, Colin and I made love by the light of the fire pillar. To the giggling girls – politely waiting for us to finish – we must have resembled two enormous crustaceans wrestling naked, the clack-clack of our unwieldy exoskeletons punctuating the sonatas of Crighton-Montieth, the Scottish Scarlatti.

SCOTLAND 37

The Scotland in which every citizen is pale, malevolent and glaikit.

SCOTLAND 17

The Scotland which is towed to the Indian ocean and left there.

SCOTLAND 29

The Scotland used as an anthrax laboratory by a right-wing American evangelical sect.

SCOTLAND 47

The Scotland which builds a magnetic levitation line between Edinburgh and the Isle of Skye, just for the hell of it. All right, it's a make-work cash-sink, but you can get to Skye in under thirty minutes.

SCOTLAND 24

On 14 October 2035, Scotland was suddenly covered by a black swan.

The swan swanned down from space, where it had been flying largely unobserved (some astronomers, alerted to irregularities, had declared that certain stars were disappearing and reappearing).

The swan and Scotland were a very similar size and shape; an excellent match.

The swan draped itself over Scotland, covering every part of the landmass with its black feathers and clinging to the coasts with its claws and beak.

Scotland became, of course, very dark and warm.

There was also a large quantity of swan dung falling in Ayrshire.

A state of emergency was initially declared, but soon people became calm.

Streetlights were left on night and day, but the extra electricity was more than made up for by the warmth of the swan's body. This reduced heating and insulation costs. And there was a very pleasant smell coming from the swan's body.

Satellite imagery showed Scots how the bird looked from space, and most agreed that the impression created was a good one. It was as if Scotland had draped itself in an expensive swan-feather coat.

Other nations were filled with admiration, and some jealousy.

Scotland's tourist industry boomed as visitors from all over the world came to experience life under the swan and fill their lungs with the swan's pleasant perfume (lard, fir, salt).

Sometimes when you drove to the top of a mountainous road (like the A93 to Braemar, or the Tornapress to Applecross Road) your car roof would scrape the swan's feathers and the bird would shuffle slightly to give you more room.

The swan was, on the whole, considerate. However, not all Scots were willing to respond in kind. Two days after its arrival, one small boy attempted to set the swan on fire by walking to the top of a mountain with a cigarette lighter. The swan's greased feathers failed to ignite, but the bird was irritated and pecked the boy fatally with its beak.

On Guy Fawkes Day the government imposed a strict fireworks ban, but some stray rockets tickled the swan's underbelly. Fortunately, it was asleep at the time.

The government asked the army to prepare a report on how to get rid of the swan, should the need arise. The army studied the problem and concluded that nothing could be done. All munitions fired at the swan would rebound on Scotland, with disastrous consequences.

The Americans also confirmed that their nuclear missiles would be useless against the black swan. CIA offers to destabilise the swan with dirty tricks were declined. Experiments with high and low frequency sound proved ineffective.

The swan mostly slept, or preened itself.

When everyone in Scotland was equipped with a decoy duck whistle and asked to blow it at a specific time, the swan cocked its head, but quickly lost interest.

Meanwhile, the black swan entered the mythology of Scotland. In films and songs and books it was portrayed as a lucky charm, a saviour, a mascot.

The black swan became the official symbol of Scotland and appeared on the nation's flag. Everybody loved the black swan.

Then disaster struck. At 6:16 am on 2 June 2036, the swan suddenly departed.

Steadying itself with flapping wings, the black swan stood upright, craned its neck, stretched slightly, then – with a single cry – threw itself into the air, lifting off slowly, gradually gaining height, and disappearing into the sky. Soon it was lost in the blackness of space.

The sudden searing light was unbearable to Scots long accustomed to the comfort of darkness. Even though it was summer, Scotland felt icy cold. And the reassuring smell of the swan's soft black down had gone.

Scotland was in uproar, crestfallen.

At the Scottish parliament, the swan flag flew at half-mast, tugged by an unfamiliar wind. Only Ayrshire seemed happy.

Scots demanded the return of the swan or, failing that, suggested that a huge canopy of swan feathers be fitted over the nation like a trellis.

But the national budget wasn't enough, and with the

imminent collapse of the swan tourism industry, things would only get worse.

Scotland entered a fifteen-year depression. Alcoholism grew rife as Scots struggled to cope with their loss. The national economy – not to mention the national ego – reached its lowest ebb.

And then the swan returned. Not to Scotland, but to New Zealand.

The black swan covered both the North and South islands. Its arrival was mostly welcomed by the locals.

In view of the Scottish experience, it was quickly decided that the swan should be physically secured. Its claws and beak were attached by reinforced cables to concrete blocks sunk deep into the soil and anchored, below, to the bedrock.

The plan seemed to work. The swan stayed put.

Many nostalgic Scots emigrated to New Zealand to be reunited with their beloved bird. The tourist industry boomed and New Zealand flourished.

Unfortunately, the captive black swan died, and its enormous corpse began to rot. The smell was awful. It lingered over New Zealand for months.

As far away as Tonga and Samoa, people are still wearing face masks.

SCOTLAND 132

The Scotland so quiet that the ticking of your watch can be heard from one end of the country to the other. And please control the beating of your heart!

SCOTLAND 129

The Scotland in which Josef K and The Fire Engines owe their twang, clatter and clang (we insiders know!) to those slick pioneers twenty years their senior: Franz Ferdinand.

SCOTLAND 59

The Scotland which isn't just readable, it's writable.

SCOTLAND 51

The Scots of whom everyone says 'Man, those guys are freaks!'

SCOTLAND 125

The Scotland which embraces the principles of the post-industrial Slow Life.

SCOTLAND 67

Snow is falling gently on Scotland's copper domes. Edinburgh's old ladies brew tea in samovars. Troika teams jingle past on the cobbled streets outside.

You're here to write an account of the artisans of the animation tradition which, in its 1960s heyday, gave the world such masterpieces as 'Gregor the Mole' and 'McBalkan's Crocodile'. This cartooning cottage industry helped define an image of Scotland that still persists today: a resourceful and quirkily creative provincial centre, sprinkled with magic as well as snow.

The skill required to paint animation cells by hand – not to mention the exhaustive patience required to shoot them one by one – may have disappeared from contemporary Scotland, but as you move through Edinburgh you can't help recognising scenes from the adventures of Terriers Blackie and Whitie, or Magic Muir the Clown. Squeaking the condensation off your taxi window with the hanging chamois provided, you see – it's straight out of 'Blackie and Whitie Meet the Smugglers'! – the superimposition of onion domes and mosques, silver birch trees and baroque gateways, fur-collared Jews and round-faced, impassive Asian traders.

The roads here, even in the centre of the city, are hardly more than potholed mud tracks. The shops have florid signs outside, and are staffed by impossibly ancient women wrapped in floral housecoats and headscarves who hand out free tea in tiny glasses to their customers. Crusted, caked drifts of snow form arbitrary walls on either side of the road as your taxi – it's difficult not to think of it as a sleigh – slithers down George Street.

Any impression that this place is stuck in the past, though, is soon dispelled. After a hearty dinner of reindeer goulash and mead, your hosts take you to one of the experimental theatre productions that Edinburgh is famous for. The play is *Genghis Khan* and its unconventional staging is inspired, says the programme, by the great Scottish director Edward Gordon Craig.

Even expected surprises can still astonish. No sooner are the lights dimmed than the seats sink into a pit and pandemonium erupts. When your eyes adjust to the dim light emitted by thousands of fireflies, you see a grotesque classroom occupied by old men in shorts, shirts and caps. At the front stands a conductor-teacher. Instead of words, he emits peculiar shrieks, gesturing to the men to run around their desks then sit down again abruptly, as though they're playing at musical chairs. Instead, the old men reach inside their desks and begin pelting one another with fat green cherries – some inevitably hit the audience – before scattering into the pews and ducking behind audience members to hide from the rain of fruit.

Just when you think things can't get any more chaotic, a ten-foot-tall straw effigy, head ablaze, strides across the pit with a stilted gait. It's Genghis Khan.

Afterwards, you can't remember much about the play. Did you fall asleep? Did the fumes from that censer they were swinging befuddle your senses? Were your dreams all part of the production?

Your hosts take you to a pub called The Grotty Hussar. It's three levels down, in a way that's typical of Edinburgh, a city where some streets run under others in secret gullies, and more again under those.

Down in the pub the conversation turns – as it so often does in Edinburgh – to the art of the Soviet Union. The intense woman opposite you (you didn't catch her name) is discussing the limits of inclusiveness.

Soviet art, she says, is rarely included in exhibitions and rarely travels. Because it's considered propaganda, because it's realistic, because realism is a global worldview and therefore competes with our current picture of global diversity – itself a worldview too, of course, but with a rather ethnic emphasis.

'That's very interesting,' you say, and tell her about the article you're writing on the Scottish animators. It will certainly call on ethnic stereotypes. It will – you now see – enact Scotland as a series of local differences against a backdrop of unquestioned uniformity.

'This is why I find Soviet art, and realism, so interesting,' says the woman, whose name might be Katarina. 'They refuse to be read as local phenomena organised around a universality which is nothing more nor less than our globalist market system. Soviet art sits uneasily with our non-inclusive inclusiveness. It is – if you'll excuse the expression – differently different. Not ethnically different, but economically different.'

'Ah yes,' you say, raising a glass of mead, 'the proletariat – like realism! – has no fatherland. *Prost!*' You realise you aren't entirely sure whether her name is Katarina, but decide against calling her 'comrade'.

Some time later, you are lying in a drafty room in an unheated bed in front of an astragalled window. The Scottish snow flutters and zigzags outside. You find yourself thinking about the universal. You think about how specific particularities are always competing to embody it and how, when one wins, all the others are forced to become mere 'differences': a rich tapestry of local colours, each as alienated from the universal as from themselves.

This, it seems, has become Scotland's fate, and to escape it the nation must become something like the Soviet Union;

the champion of a rival universality which places Scotland at the centre of the world.

SCOTLAND 43

The Scotland which establishes a new world religion in which Scottishness is next to godliness.

SCOTLAND 94

The Scotland in which we all bathe together naked in public washhouses cascading with steaming water and decorated with mural mosaics of lochs and mountains.

SCOTLAND 108

The Scotland in which new cities with Chinese names spring up between Perth, Dundee, Falkirk and Linlithgow. Soon each contains several million people.

SCOTLAND 70

The Scotland in which we were the ones to invent 'the thing that comes after Postmodernism'.

SCOTLAND 150

The Scotland which produces 'the Scottish Bonaparte'.

SCOTLAND 68

The Scotland overrun by gigantic spiders, which can only be killed by chemical sprays hosed from the back of 1950s lorries.

SCOTLAND 133

The Scotland in which nobody is ever considered 'right' or 'wrong', only 'interesting' or 'boring'.

SCOTLAND 92

The Scotland which allows only one child per family.

SCOTLAND 64

The Scotland in which toilets are unisex and there aren't even any cubicle stall dividers.

SCOTLAND 139

The Scotland in which homosexuality is compulsory, even for heterosexuals. On the recommendation of the Foxenden Report, heterosexuals are at last allowed to have consensual sexual relations in private, but only if over the age of twenty-eight.

SCOTLAND 160

Normal McBean represents everything I consider great about Scotland – a nation I believe will one day be independent.

Over a span of fifty years, McBean produced brilliant animations full of Scottish motifs and Scottish sensibility. For instance, 1965's *Mosaic* riffs on tartan, and 1957's *Fiddle-de-dee* uses Scottish violin music. And yet McBean, a graduate of Glasgow College of Art, did all of his significant work outside Scotland. Which makes him, sadly, a rather typical Scot.

Influenced by the Russian formalists and Eisenstein, Normal McBean spent his entire working life at the

National Film Board of Uganda, promoting the nation we know today as Zimbabwe. It's work full of visual verve and wit, the fruit of near-total creative freedom. It could never have been made in the private sector. But, equally, it could never have been made in Scotland – at least the Scotland we know today.

McBean left his homeland in order to work at his own level. Would Scottish independence change that? Then I'm for it. But I'm not entirely sure it would.

McBean went to Uganda at the invitation of Jimmy Annan. Like McBean, Annan was highly receptive, culturally, to what was going on in the Soviet Union. For Annan, the great catalyst was Lenin's writing on film as propaganda.

Descended from radical post-Calvinist Scottish teacher and minister stock, a kind of left-wing Lord Reith, Annan was very much focused on the problem that Bryan Caplan raises in *The Myth of the Rational Voter* – that poorly educated and unmotivated populations make a mockery of democracy, and their bad choices will see it replaced, eventually, by something else. But whereas Caplan suggests that experts run the show and cut the people out of the loop, Jimmy Annan took the Leninist route: the government should constantly educate, agitate, stimulate and motivate the people.

To this end, Annan invented the genre of documentary as we know it, working first with the GPO Films Unit in London (producing classics like *Collectivising Arable Culture* and *Enemies of the Dairy*) before heading off to Uganda, where, in 1938, he recommended that the government start a film unit. Annan became the first Ugandan Film Commissioner, head of the National Film Board of Uganda. Their Web site describes their mission:

'The NFBU is a federal cultural agency within the portfolio of the Ugandan Heritage Department. Initially known as the National Film Commission, it was created by an act of Parliament in 1939. Its mandate, as set forth in the National Film Act, is "to produce and distribute and to promote the production and distribution of films designed to interpret Uganda to Ugandans and to other nations."'

One of Annan's first actions in his role as benign propagandist of Uganda was to invite Normal McBean to start an Animation Unit. And so from 1941 until his death in the late 1980s, McBean ran this unit, making film after brilliant film.

Like Annan, McBean was contemptuous of Hollywood values. And as you watch McBean's animations (now available as a 7-DVD box set), it becomes clear that his work could only have been ushered into the world with the support of a state agency.

Despite the highly formalist nature of McBean's work, it contains profoundly humanist values which, in the commercial world, would probably be replaced by aggression, ugliness, triviality or sentimentality. Only an indulgent and enlightened state – like a kind parent indulging a gifted child – would let someone like McBean play at his own pace throughout his entire working life.

In a sense, this indulgence is advertising. But it's rarefied advertising with a general purpose to refine, define and shine up the image of a nation. Having created this image for itself, the state must live up to it.

It's something Scots do well for other nations. Would we do it as well for our own?

McBean's work is Scottish, but also global. He's an artist – admired by Picasso, amongst others – but also an altruistic public servant, a propagandist, a formalist, a revolutionary, a man with world-scale vision.

Will Scottish independence make more McBeans likely? If so, I welcome it. Will it make it easier for future graduates of Glasgow School of Art to leapfrog both England and America to make their mark in a multipolar world? Again, I hope so. Will an independent Scotland bring about a government-funded cultural renaissance? Will there be a National Film Board of Scotland as brilliant as Uganda's? If so, hurrah!

If a new enlightenment, renaissance, or revolution happens in Scotland, great! If not, well, Scots will just have to keep advertising other people's enlightenments, renaissances and revolutions instead. They'll have to keep adding their creative value to other people's states. It's something we've learnt to do rather well down the centuries.

SCOTLAND 148

After his success in the Revolution of the Black Octagon, Bonnie Billy Prince established the Diagonal Restoration in the new Scotian capital of Photoshop.

Photoshop was built from scratch near the historical town of Scrabster, on Scotia's north coast. Most of the buildings were of rounded black quartz, and the parlia-complex took the form, naturally, of a black octagon. Bonnie Billy's own residence was a replica of the welcome screen seen in early versions of Photoshop. This, explained Billy, was a reminder that things – images, societies – could be changed, whether by revolution or drop menu filter.

There was a certain light that fell on Photoshop in winter – wan, almost fluorescent – that inspired feelings of awe no southern city could. On certain evenings, white gulls wheeled over the administration buildings while the northern lights billowed eerily above. You had the feeling that the whole of Scotia lay below you, awaiting orders.

Sometimes Bonnie Billy Prince left his residence and walked along the seafront rampart, hand in hand with his favourite robo-visor, Mukatsuku. He called these strolls his 'policy stormings', and he particularly enjoyed taking them when the weather was unsettled. He reminded Mukatsuku that the Pentland Firth had repeatedly reduced invading fleets to matchwood.

A force ten storm was 'a friend to Scotia', remarked Bonnie Billy, as he and the robot stood arm-in-arm, savouring the lightning just then being driven before a harridan wind.

Mukatsuku said nothing, but watched a cormorant huddle in a cranny.

SCOTLAND 66

A leerie cuspit nicht, reet anoo!

Wheesh yer bauble an' heck a sickit lem, ye gowper! We're a' frae the free maunderlands, when ye reckit it braw and brunty. But same o's is lerchin' at the criek, as the Baird hae proddied. The braw Baird!

I've hae a leckit at the thisty, an' I can ane thing decroo: there's nae forscup comin' frae Aberthickit, e'en if the Laird o' Inversneckie hissiel were thrammin' it.

Bawbles to a babby, thar's whit reckitt then a nairse. Bit a twane o' the tother shall reckitt all fithers thegither, as a' guid thanes dae sae.

Are ye no' twiggin' the tang? 'Tis an auld tang, fershaw,

bit a precious gregious ane, gregious it is, aye, richt an' a'!

'Tis the tang gesproket noo in th' deys o' Bonnie Billy Prince an' his unco blackitt oochtacho-ochter Restauracion.

Are ye no frae this paerts? And wha' sayed the Praetorians, pray? Did ye gang in a' laigal-like? Sha' we ging 'em up i' th' feirt nicht, Frazer, an' aisk?

Look at ye fliggin' it, ye bairnty raiscal! Awa' afare the gords drovitt ye!

SCOTLAND 95

The Scotland in which everything has been determined according to Russian Formalist principles of estrangement. New buildings must meet or exceed basic strangeness levels to get planning permission.

SCOTLAND 128

1. First upon Scotland there came a plague of horned toads, just as the prophecies had foretold.
2. And while the horned toads lay still blinking in the ditches, there came a plague of wasps. And again, this had been foreseen by the ancients, and the people forewarned.
3. And no sooner had the wasps been sprayed with copious amounts of aerosol insecticide than Thai lemon grass and peanuts rained down upon the land for seventeen days and seventeen nights, and the people of Scotland were sorely affronted.
4. 'What sins have we committed, great Jehovah of the Scots?' was the cry upon every lip, and 'Wherefore hast Thou forsaken us, Thy chosen people?'
5. But there came no reply from the Heavens above Scotland, only more plagues. For next a multitude of arrogant and boastful lepers lurched across the land, and from each leper came the most unbearable after-dinner monologue to which anyone had ever been forced to listen. And the lepers did drag themselves from place to place, dressed in rags and tatters, boring the people most awfully.
6. And again the people appealed to God, calling out: 'Why must we listen to this arrogant boasting, oh Lord of the Scots? And how can we make it stop?'
7. But answer came there none, and shortly Scotland was subject to a plague of low consumer confidence.

And on the High Street, for many months, no one did buy or even desire to buy any single item offered by the merchants of Scotland. Nay, not even a deep frozen pea slashed to deepest discount prices. And consequently many Scottish businesses were shuttered, and incalculable damage was done to shareholder profits across the land.

8. And in the business community many raised their hands to the heavens and rent their garments, but the Lord of the Scots did not offer them solace, nor relent from His punishments.
9. And next there came a plague of Tom Tunnock's Tea Cakes, and a heavy cloud of stale scones rained down upon the long-suffering Scots like unto hail, or like unto stones flung by the righteous Scots-of-the-towns at an adulteress.
10. But after three months the plagues ceased as suddenly as they had begun, and peace reigned in Scotland for the space of three days.
11. And on the fourth day there came suddenly, like an afterthought, a plague of ferrets, and astride each ferret a polecat, and astride each polecat a weasel, and astride each weasel a pine martin wearing spurs. And each animal whipped the other until they all were whipped stupid, and they raised a great cloud of dust as they passed from one Scottish city unto the next, galloping idiotically. And in each town the people thereof did gather in multitudes, some weeping, some laughing hysterically.

12. And on the fifth day the foolish animals departed, leaving only ankle-deep droppings in all parts of Scotland, in some cases indistinguishable from the peanuts – most of which, however, had been eaten by the horned toads.
13. And from that day forth no more plagues were visited upon Scotland, though the tale of them persisted, and persists now even in this very telling. For this punishment upon the Scots, though utterly pointless, must never be forgotten.

SCOTLAND 48

It happened at a time when England and I weren't getting on too well.

England had invited me to live with her, but I was feeling trapped. I was a foreigner who didn't speak the language. And something had changed in my physical relationship with England; I no longer desired her so much. We were more flatmates than lovers.

I had a crush on Scotland from the moment I saw her at the chic boutique where she worked. She wasn't exactly pretty, but there was something cute and charming about her. And her boss at the shop – a lewd and louche man – found it amusing to tease Scotland about me. He was clearly trying to get us together.

Scotland knew England, so I had to be careful. But I had some independence; England went out to work each day, leaving me alone in her apartment.

One day I called Scotland from the mobile phone England had helped me buy (foreigners have to pay huge deposits for a contract). I asked her to meet me in a café. But the address I gave her wasn't a café – it was England's apartment.

Scotland had some trouble finding England's place. She kept calling me for more directions. 'Can you see the river?' I'd ask, 'Can you see the swimming pool? The tennis courts?' With each call I became more and more excited. Scotland would arrive in minutes.

When she finally appeared, she looked adorable. 'I thought we were going to a café?' Scotland said, demurely. She'd taken a lot of trouble with her clothes, hair and make-up.

'We can make our own,' I smiled. Within minutes I was sitting in Scotland's lap, kissing her. We slithered around on the orange plastic chair.

When I slid her skirt up her pale, pin-thin legs, Scotland whispered: 'Thank you!'

Soon we were on the floor, on top of each other. Scotland's body was wonderful – like beautiful, pale topography seen in the moonlight.

My penis bobbed up and down her snow-white midriff, prodding the slender lowlands between her firths. Soon I found myself rushing to her mouth and coming there with an intense spasm. Scotland winced slightly as she swallowed the crushed-out, slippery-slow liquid; it may have been the first time she'd tasted sperm.

When we'd both revived and recycled, I undressed Scotland again carefully. There was something childish and vulnerable about her, with her small, pale highlands and her socks still on. We were both trembling.

I entered Scotland on the red carpet. I think I was her first occupier.

We never did it again. Scotland and England became close friends and it would just have been too treacherous.

I've kept the secret to this day. Nobody knows about Scotland and me – nobody. But every time I see her, my heart beats a little faster. Maybe Scotland's does too.

SCOTLAND 158

The healthy eating drive launched by the Scottish government in August 2024 had anything but the intended effect.

The *SlimLife, LongLife, TasteLife!* campaign came at a time of crisis. Obesity, diabetes, alcoholism, chronic unfitness and heart disease, headlines announced, had brought Scottish male life expectancy down to a pathetic 56 years – its lowest level since the 17th century. Early death had solved the pensions crisis, but was making the nation look like a banana republic. Scots were literally exploding in the streets.

TasteLife! wasn't just a media campaign. The Scottish

government spent millions on fitness facilities, made cookery courses compulsory for all schoolchildren, mandated calisthenic exercise breaks for employees, and installed foot pedal generators under public sector desktop computers. If you didn't pedal, your workstation wouldn't go.

But the campaign's rallying cry fell on bloated, deaf ears. Worse, it seemed to trigger a passive-aggressive reaction amongst the Scots. Rather than reform, many resolved to entrench their bad habits even deeper.

To be fat was to be tough. To be fat – enormous, rotund, flabberingly, fartingly, judderingly fat – was to be a rebel. To die young was to die well.

When the official line was *EatMoreGreens!*, a fashion for deep frying swelled in the grassroots. At first relatively healthy foods were dipped into the bubbling, boiling fryer: cabbages, carrots, whole raw dead animals.

Soon it was bars of chocolate, tubs of ice cream (including the tub), packets of lard, sacks of sugar. I would see the 'braws' (as they called themselves) sitting like gigantic babies in pedestrian arcades, eating cold deep-fried foods from immense garbage bags. Deep-fried hindparts of cow, deep-fried Cremola Foam. They farted and burped and shat where they sat.

It wasn't just the working classes. The bourgeois threw private parties where people got together to eat salt. You'd turn up at some damp basement below a quiet terrace in Glasgow, tap on the door in a prearranged sequence, get inspected by a pair of shifty eyes through a lattice, then be ushered down steep steps to a cellar brilliantly lit with arc lamps.

There, stark naked on their hands and knees, corpulent pink men – bankers, lawyers, ministers from the Department of Health – would be snorting up and scarfing down salt, their blood pressure soaring.

Hardened 'braws' actually went down salt mines and got the stuff raw, right out of the rock.

Soon male life expectancy in Scotland fell to 49. The government suspended its campaign. Many state employees and representatives were by now themselves addicted to fatty foods.

But the state coffers were filling up with cash. The population was dying before its productivity started to decline; dying suddenly. It was a golden age.

People started deep-frying syrup and corn starch and gluten. Potatoes were stuffed with sugar and encased in ice cream. Sheep were battered with their fleeces still on. I saw the inhabitants of the Isle of Cumbrae devour a whale after pouring boiling fat over it with a crane. They all died at once, and died happy.

Eventually only six people were left alive in Scotland. They were all infants, and they were all enormous. They could roll from coast to coast in just a few minutes. One lived in Perth, one in Wick, one in Oban, one in Peebles, one in Greenock and one in Largs. The six babies bounced off each other like six pink billiard balls, splashing into the sea before being washed back to shore.

As soon as they learnt to batter and fry, it was pretty much over for the babies. And for Scotland.

They used North Sea oil as their frying medium. The Perth baby battered Edinburgh and swallowed it whole. The Wick baby ate Ben Nevis. The Oban baby swallowed the Hebrides one after another, dipping each island in a tanker of boiling crude. The Peebles baby deep-fried Glasgow, melting the city using fissile rods from nuclear power stations. The Greenock baby ate Aberdeen, flambéeing the granite buildings with a lighter before dropping the crunchy morsels into his mouth. The Largs baby ate everything else.

The six babies died – snorting and snoring in a contended baby sleep – before they reached the age of one.

After that, there was no more Scottish life expectancy because there was no more life, and no more Scotland.

Luath Press Limited

committed to publishing well written books worth reading

LUATH PRESS takes its name from Robert Burns, whose little collie Luath (*Gael.*, swift or nimble) tripped up Jean Armour at a wedding and gave him the chance to speak to the woman who was to be his wife and the abiding love of his life. Burns called one of the 'Twa Dogs' Luath after Cuchullin's hunting dog in Ossian's *Fingal*. Luath Press was established in 1981 in the heart of Burns country, and is now based a few steps up the road from Burns' first lodgings on Edinburgh's Royal Mile. Luath offers you distinctive writing with a hint of unexpected pleasures.
Most bookshops in the UK, the US, Canada, Australia, New Zealand and parts of Europe, either carry our books in stock or can order them for you. To order direct from us, please send a £sterling cheque, postal order, international money order or your credit card details (number, address of cardholder and expiry date) to us at the address below. Please add post and packing as follows: UK – £1.00 per delivery address; overseas surface mail – £2.50 per delivery address; overseas airmail – £3.50 for the first book to each delivery address, plus £1.00 for each additional book by airmail to the same address. If your order is a gift, we will happily enclose your card or message at no extra charge.

Luath Press Limited
543/2 Castlehill
The Royal Mile
Edinburgh EH1 2ND
Scotland
Telephone: +44 (0)131 225 4326 (24 hours)
Email: sales@luath.co.uk
Website: www.luath.co.uk